Still Crazy

Still Crazy

Dick Clement

and

Ian La Frenais

SCREENPRESS BOOKS

First published in 1998
by ScreenPress Books
28 Castle Street Eye Suffolk IP23 7AW

Photoset by Parker Typesetting Service, Leicester
Printed in England by Clays Ltd, St Ives plc

A CIP record for this book
is available from the British Library

ISBN 1 901680 21 5

For more information on forthcoming ScreenPress Books,
contact the publishers at:

ScreenPress Books
28 Castle Street
Eye Suffolk
IP23 7AW
or fax on: 01379 870 261

10 9 8 7 6 5 4 3 2 1

Contents

Introduction

Three main reasons encouraged us to write *Still Crazy*. One is our affection for music and musicians. Another is the poignancy of people whose lives peak too early. And the third is our belief that even in middle age it's possible to recapture a passion for something that shaped your life years ago.

The genesis of the idea came from a member of a famous 1960s rock band who told us what happened when they re-formed for a reunion tour several years later: 'Half an hour in the dressing room at the first gig of the tour was enough to remind us all why we broke up in the first place.'

Before we could start the screenplay, we sat down to invent the band and their history. We called this our 'sleeve notes'. It put them into historical perspective and gave us a sense of their triumphs and disasters, their rise and ultimate fall. We even wrote two record reviews by John Peel which epitomized two crucial moments in their career. He described their seminal album, *Sonic Handshake*, as 'a superb mélange of sleek roots-rock groove and post-Beatles psychedelia'. (The album outsold T. Rex's *Electric Warrior*, but the single was kept out of the No. 1 slot by Benny Hill's 'Ernie, Fastest Milkman in the West'.) Some years later, in their metally period, Peel had to report, more sadly, that the Fruits' new album, *Tequila Mockingbird*, was 'a robotic simulation of their early efforts, amorphous, campy and depressing'. The Fruits weren't sure what 'amorphous' meant, but they knew it wasn't good, and a few months later the Sex Pistols punted them into oblivion.

In between these two extremes the guys sat in their air-conditioned land yachts and their tinted limos, traversing the archetypal landscape of rock 'n' roll: fame, fornication, fatality, fortune, friction and failure.

While we were always very specific about the Fruits' history (first gig, Peterborough Polytechnic, 5 September 1969), we were always a little vague about the kind of music they actually played. When the film became a reality, it was time to deal with this. In the recording studio Clive Langer, Alan Winstanley and a group of accomplished session musicians defined their sound, and became enthusiastic arbiters of what was Fruits and what was not. A riff, even a whole song, would be rejected if, in their opinion, 'It wasn't Fruity enough.'

Four years after we started this venture, the Fruits are finally on film. We have Amanda Marmot to thank for her resilience, her persistence and her unshaking belief in the project. And Brian Gibson, who kept pushing us to improve the script, just as he later pushed his cast and, more than anyone, himself. And, finally, the actors who brought each character so vividly to life.

Even if the film had not been made, the Fruits would never have left us. They'd become our friends, our family. We laughed at their antics, despaired at their ego-fuelled stupidities. And we were both convinced that if we went into the dark closets where our wives consign all our old stuff, there, among the afghan coats, the Biggles books, the Rupert annuals and the unstrung tennis racquets, would be a cardboard box of vinyl albums – and at least three of them would be by Strange Fruit.

Dick Clement and Ian La Frenais,
October 1998

Still Crazy

Over black, under presentation credits, we hear the voice of Hughie:

HUGHIE

History teaches us that men behave wisely once they've exhausted all other alternatives. For most rock bands the pursuit of wisdom is a low priority compared to fame, fortune and fornication. Such a band was Strange Fruit . . .

As the actors' credits are shown we begin to hear the sound of a backstage row:

LES

(*voice-over*)

You told us this was an important gig, Neil.

NEIL

(*voice-over*)

It *is* an important gig.

BEANO

(*voice-over*)

It's a waterlogged fucking field, miles from anywhere.

HUGHIE

(*voice-over*)

I was their road-dog twenty years ago, when they played the Wisbech Rock Festival . . .

NEIL

(*voice-over*)

Look, lads, there's twenty thousand fans out there waiting to see you.

BEANO

(*voice-over*)

Only 'cause they can't go anywhere . . . They're up to their bollocks in mud.

TONY

(*voice-over*)

I think we should sing 'Painted Lady' as a tribute to Keith.

RAY

(*voice-over*)

Why? What's the point?

TONY

(*voice-over*)

Well, it's two years since he, y'know, passed on.

RAY

(*voice-over*)

He didn't pass on. He OD'd in a Little Chef!

NEIL

(*voice-over*)

Nice thought, Tony, but it would bring everybody down, y'know.

LES

(*voice-over*)

Never mind what we play, it's *when* we play. You guaranteed us we'd close the night!

NEIL

(*voice-over*)

No, I didn't, Les. I guaranteed you'd go on after Blodwyn Pig and Uriah Heep.

RAY

(*voice-over*)

And what about Mott the Hoople?

NEIL

(*voice-over*)

Can't move that, it's a done deal.

TONY

(*voice-over*)

We're the Fruits, Neil, we're the Fruits, man!

HUGHIE

(*voice-over*)

And you should be on-stage!

LES

(*voice-over*)

Without Brian?

NEIL

(*voice-over*)

Oh, God. Where the fuck is he? And where's Karen?!

RAY

(*voice-over*)

It's a question of stature. You have to consider where we stand in the overall spectrum.

NEIL

(*voice-over*)

So where do we, Ray?

RAY

(*voice-over*)

W-well, above Mott the fucking Hoople, surely.

NEIL

(*voice-over*)

They're on at three in the morning, no one will be awake . . .

Credits end and pictures.

Fade in:

EXT. WISBECH ROCK FESTIVAL. BACKSTAGE. NIGHT

Strange Fruit is a typical 1970s rock band: pasty-faced, slightly wasted, masses of hair and skinny – with the exception of the drummer, Beano. They're arguing with their manager, Neil.

NEIL

Lindisfarne went on in daylight!

BEANO

So they should. They're fuckin' folk singers.

Karen, eighteen, with long dark hair, appears with Brian. His face is a mixture of mischief and innocence – and he's more than slightly stoned.

NEIL

Oh, what's he on, horse tranquillizers? You're supposed to be looking after him, Karen!

KAREN

I've never let him out of my sight.

NEIL

Forget about the album and all the negative press stuff. Go out there and remind them what the Fruits were – are . . . WILL BE!

EXT. WISBECH ROCK FESTIVAL. AUDITORIUM. NIGHT

The crowd are getting restless. Some of them are putting on raincoats, eyeing the sky above. There's an ominous rumble of thunder.

PA ANNOUNCEMENT

You've been very patient. but it's worth waiting for. I know you want to hear the guys, so let's hear it for – STRANGE FRUIT!!!

The band walk on-stage, Tony to the keyboards, Beano to the drums. Brian and Les sling their guitars. A few cheers and some derisive jeers. Ray appears to an equally mixed reception. He sulks his way to the mike.

Beano starts to kick in the beat. 'One, two, three, four . . .' The band kick in. Ray picks up the mike stand and starts to sing 'All Those Dangerous Things':

RAY

'Watch where you turn, it might be today-ay-yeay . . .'

He looks at Brian. He's playing a different tempo, might be on another planet. Ray yells at him.

'You lose your head, then just throw it away . . .'

There's an enormous crash of thunder and lightning forks on to the stage. The set ends in chaos. As the band leave the stage, we hear:

HUGHIE

(*voice-over*)

It was their last gig. Divine intervention pulled the plug on the Fruits. God just got sick of all that 1970s excess. That's why he invented the Sex Pistols.

Hughie takes Brian's guitar. As Tony leaves the stage, he mutters:

TONY

That ought to tell us something . . .

Dissolve to:

EXT. SPANISH PORT. DAY

A small port, under Mediterranean sunshine. A caption reads: '1998'. A small car pulls up.

Tony Costello gets out of a ten-year-old Seat and grabs a bulging briefcase from the back seat. He wears aviator shades and tight, faded jeans. He heads for the nearest bar.

HUGHIE

(*voice-over*)

So the band went their separate ways, dragging their dwindling royalties and bruised egos behind them. Tony sold his Yamaha but he still puts 'rock star' as his job description. Though for the last few years no one's been quite sure what it is he actually does . . .

As Tony is about to enter the bar a young man recognizes him – Steve Greenblatt, about twenty-eight, Jewish, with curly hair, sitting with a girl at an outside table.

STEVE

Tony Costello?

TONY

Maybe. Who's asking?

STEVE

Strange Fruit, right? Steve Greenblatt. Big fan, Tony. That's amazing. My dad put on the Wisbech Rock Festival!

TONY

No kidding?

STEVE

Can I buy you a drink?

TONY

Er, sure. I just have a spot of business first.

STEVE

Oh, you live here? Retired to the sun, eh? Lucky you.

INT. BAR. MEN'S ROOM. DAY

The barman watches as Tony opens his briefcase, propped on a washbasin. Is this a drug deal going down?

TONY

How's business?

BARMAN

Slow. The English aren't here.

Tony unlocks a vending machine selling condoms. It's almost full. He reacts with dismay.

TONY

Bloody hell, things are slow!

He starts to restock it.

INT. THE VIKING HOTEL. LOBBY. DAY

It's a new building, like a Posthouse or a Holiday Inn, which caters mostly for business conferences and seminars, somewhere north-west of London.

Karen descends an escalator. She wears a pleated skirt, white shirt and pale blue blazer.

HUGHIE

(*voice-over*)

Karen still had ink on her fingers from school when she went to work for the Fruits. Started by sorting their laundry, and by Wisbech was sorting their lives.

EXT. WISBECH ROCK FESTIVAL. BACKSTAGE. NIGHT

The band are arguing as they leave the stage in the rain. Brian slips off the edge of the duckboard and falls on his arse in the mud.

Karen turns back and helps him to his feet. He has a folorn, sweet, stoned smile on his mud-spattered face. She takes off her scarf and starts cleaning it up. And the rain pounds down on both of them . . .

HUGHIE

(*voice-over*)

'Course, they treated her like crap, but she loved the music and idolized Brian. The wee bastard was a near-genius, but he was hell-bent on going the same way as his brother, Keith, already dead from a drug overdose.

INT. THE VIKING HOTEL. LOBBY. DAY

Karen moves into the hotel lobby, which is filled with conference delegates wearing name-tags.

HUGHIE

(*voice-over*)

So she did a complete one-eighty – marriage and a mortgage, a daughter and divorce.

KAREN

Gentlemen, my name is Karen Knowles. Welcome to the Viking Hotel, your conference centre home-from-home. You're all set up in the Collingwood Suite. You'll find tea, coffee, leaded and unleaded, and lunch will be served at twelve-thirty.

MALE EXECUTIVE

Brilliant, Karen. I'll buy you a drink later. The Admiral's Locker at six?

He doesn't even wait for a reply, giving her a confident pat on the bum.

INT. HOTEL MANAGER'S OFFICE. DAY

Karen is confronting her boss, Kevin, a few years younger and a few inches shorter than her.

KEVIN

He brings a dozen conferences a year here. I'd like to give him the benefit of the doubt.

KAREN

He tries it on every time.

KEVIN

Karen, what this job needs is a people pleaser. Sometimes I think you don't even like people.

KAREN

(*as she exits*)

What? So pleasing people is letting them touch my arse?

INT. HOTEL LOBBY. DAY

Karen leaves Kevin's office, still steaming. Someone else touches her on the arm. She whirls round – now what? It's Tony, looking out of place among the suits.

TONY

Hi, babe. What's happening?

Karen can't believe her eyes.

KAREN

Tony?

INT. LATER. HOTEL LOBBY. DAY

As Kevin walks through the busy lobby, looking for Karen, we hear:

TONY

(*voice-over*)

. . . and it turns out he's the son of the original promoter of the Wisbech Rock Festival.

We see Karen sitting opposite Tony.

KAREN

Wisbech?

TONY

Anyway, he wants to set it up again. Putting on some of the original acts.

KAREN

And he wants the Fruits.

Kevin catches Karen's eye across a stairwell and indicates that she's needed.

I'm at work, Tony. What is it you want?

TONY

I've no idea how to track the lads down. I could use a bit of help.

Kevin appears, glancing at Tony – who the hell is he? Tony gives him a laid-back wave.

Hi!

KEVIN

Karen, the Mitsubishi delegates are wandering around reception like lost sheep.

KAREN

I'm on my way . . .

Kevin leaves.

You can't really see this happening, can you, Tony? You all hated each other at the end.

TONY

Hate's a bit heavy. Look, I just need some phone numbers. I owe it to the guys to at least let them know about it. Some of them may not be doing so well.

KAREN

They were desperate times, best forgotten. I've had enough rock 'n' roll to last a lifetime.

Tony looks around the hotel and calls after Karen:

TONY

So you gave it all up for this?

EXT. BUILDING SITE. DAY

A cold, grey day outside a building where restoration work is in progress. Tony appears. He looks apprehensively up a ladder and starts to climb . . .

EXT. ROOFTOP. DAY

Les Wickes is hard at work on the apex of the roof, the wind whipping at his face, a mobile phone clipped to his belt. He looks like he's worked out of doors a long time.

Tony's face appears above the guttering. The climb hasn't helped his confidence.

TONY

Les!

Les turns in surprise to see Tony.

HUGHIE

(*voice-over*)

Les Wickes was the most pissed off when the band broke up . . .

EXT. STAGE. NIGHT

The young Les, playing bass guitar, glaring at Ray.

HUGHIE

(*voice-over*)

. . . mind, he'd been pissed off ever since Keith died and Ray Simms replaced him. Now he swears he doesn't miss it . . . Well, his wife believes him . . .

EXT. ROOFTOP. DAY

LES

Tony!

TONY

Hi, man!

Les gets up. A wider shot reveals the two of them on the roof of a church.

LES

There's only two reasons you'd haul your arse up here. Either I owe you money . . .

TONY

Or?

LES

Or you want to put the band together.

TONY

We had a shot, man. A real shot for greatness. Don't tell me it hasn't haunted you all these years.

LES

No. Just glad I got out when I did and built up a decent business.

TONY

That's Camille talking.

His foot dislodges a tile, which slides down the roof. He looks down apprehensively.

Is it trickier getting down?

EXT. BUILDING SITE. DAY

Les descends the long ladder with Tony slung over his shoulder like someone rescued from a fire.

TONY

You wanted it as much as any of us. Money, hit records, being famous. Don't tell me this is a step up, Les . . .

INT. KAREN'S HOUSE. GARAGE. NIGHT

Karen squats on the floor of her overcrowded garage, rummaging through an old chest.

Her teenage daughter, Clare, enters.

CLARE

Mum?

KAREN

(*startled*)

You frightened the life out of me!

CLARE

What are you doing?

KAREN

Look at all this stuff! Should've thrown it out years ago.

CLARE

So why didn't you?

KAREN

I thought you might like to wear these.

She holds up a pair of platform-heel shoes. Clare laughs and leaves.

Karen puts the shoes back in the trunk. We see what she's been looking at – a scrapbook of the Fruits. She touches one of the photographs.

Dissolve to:

INT. BACKSTAGE. NIGHT

Close on a guitar, picking out a tune. It's played by the younger Brian, using a sixpence for a pick. Karen sits listening, totally entranced, beguiled by Brian and the beautiful music he's making. He looks at Karen, laughs, and hands the sixpence towards her.

INT. LAUNDERETTE. LONDON. DAY

Tony is the only male customer, reading Mojo. *A phone rings inside his pocket. He fumbles for it.*

TONY

Costello Music . . .

KAREN

(*voice-over*)

Tony, it's me.

TONY

Karen!

KAREN

(*voice-over*)

I . . . I've just handed in my notice.

TONY

(*brightening*)

You're in? . . . Fantastic, man!

INT. KAREN'S CAR. DAY

Karen is driving with Tony beside her. Through trees they glimpse a house – large, dark and Gothic.

TONY

I can't believe he hung on to this pile.

KAREN

Ray was always careful with his money.

TONY

And I'm dossing down in my sister's council flat! The only thing I have of value is this.

He fingers a locket around his neck.

KAREN

What is it?

Tony opens it and produces a brown-stained molar. Karen recoils but Tony looks at it with reverence.

TONY

Jimi Hendrix's tooth! There was a fight in a club on Oxford Street. Someone planked him and I picked it up . . . I knew he was a genius, even then.

KAREN

And you think it would fetch you a fortune at Sotheby's?

TONY

Oh, absolutely. No two ways about it.

Karen is not so sure.

EXT. RAY'S HOUSE. DRIVEWAY. DAY

Karen slows the Renault as they turn into the driveway. They react on seeing about thirty cars parked on both sides.

KAREN

What's going on here?

INT. RAY'S HOUSE. RECEPTION ROOM. DAY

Close on a toastmaster in a formal red coat.

TOASTMASTER

Ladies and gentlemen, a toast, by our host, the father of the bride!

Wider angle reveals a wedding reception taking place. The sombre figure of Ray Simms gets to his feet. He wears dark glasses and platform shoes, in sharp contrast to the groom's family in their formal wear and thatched hats. He takes the mike.

RAY

Testing, one two, one two!

EXT. STAGE. NIGHT

A quick flash of Ray as he used to be on-stage, strutting his stuff.

INT. RAY'S HOUSE. RECEPTION ROOM. DAY

RAY

Hello, Wembley!

The guests look blank, not getting his little joke.

As you know, I'm a man of music. And Tamsin is a child of song . . .

Karen and Tony enter at the back of the room, taking in what they've walked in on.

. . . And I must say she remains one of the best songs I ever wrote . . .

KAREN

I think our timing's a bit off.

RAY

. . . Er, or I should say, rather, *co*-wrote, with her mother, June . . .

Ray's ex-wife, a lady in blue, looks suitably satisfied that a near-slight has been averted.

. . . who we're lucky enough to have with us here today.

Tony and Karen stand next to two middle-aged waitresses.

FIRST WAITRESS

What was the name of that band he was in?

RAY

(*off-screen*)

I don't write speeches, I write lyrics . . .

SECOND WAITRESS

I've been trying to remember. It's driving me crazy.

TONY

Strange Fruit.

They hadn't realized Tony was standing behind them. They stare at him.

FIRST WAITRESS

Strange . . .?

TONY

Fruit.

We go back to Ray as he checks a piece of paper, his prepared speech.

RAY

. . . I'd like to read you these, taken from my first solo album, *Taking Wing.*

Coughs and shuffling feet as everyone wonders what's coming.

'Love is the heat that melts the wax of wings . . . Fly close to that heat, dear child, fly close . . .

The guests look bewildered. Karen and Tony exchange 'Can you believe this?' looks.

. . . For when the smoke clears, what remains? The sweet kissing breath of lips and thighs . . . And sky-blue eyes – that love!'

Ray sits down to bemused applause. Tony knocks over a large vase of flowers with a crash. Ray reacts to the sound, removing his shades. He's startled to see Karen and Tony. They give a self-conscious wave.

EXT. RAY'S HOUSE. COURTYARD. DAY

Ray steers Karen and Tony across the courtyard.

TONY

We'd have called, but obviously you're ex-directory.

RAY

No, it's cool, really, it's cool. Why don't we talk in the crypt?

INT. RAY'S HOUSE. RECORDING STUDIO. DAY

Ray listens as Karen explains the reason for their visit.

KAREN

The thing is, Tony's trying to get the Fruits together for a reunion gig.

RAY

Really? Have you spoken to Les?

TONY

We, er . . . we wanted to talk to you first. Naturally.

RAY

There was always complex *karma* between him and me. From the moment I joined the band.

KAREN

Long time ago, Ray. We've all moved on, I'm sure.

TONY

He said you were a wanker, but he always thought you had a good set of pipes.

Ray isn't sure if this is a compliment or not.

The door opens and Astrid enters. Her Swedish accent is as strong as it was when she left Malmö eighteen years ago.

ASTRID

Ray, please, what do you do in here?

KAREN

Hello, Astrid. Karen, remember? And Tony?

ASTRID

Oh, hello. I am forgetting. Did we invite you?

RAY

They're putting the Fruits together, Astrid.

ASTRID

(*shocked*)

Why would you want to?

TONY

A lot of outfits are surfing the nostalgia wave. Cleaning up, some of them.

ASTRID

Ray is in the middle of a solo album. We work night and day.

TONY

We?

ASTRID

Ray play every instrument. Sometimes I make percussion on tinker bells. And we are our own back-up vocals. It is very happening 'now' music. Strange Fruit are passé, they are an old hat.

Ray would like to disagree but can't find the words.

EXT. RAY'S HOUSE. COURTYARD. DAY

Astrid and Ray watch from the doorway as Karen and Tony leave.

TONY

(*gloomily*)

Without a lead singer we're bollixed.

KAREN

Astrid said no, not Ray. Remember, his last solo album was in '89.

TONY

I'm dying for a pee. Hang on . . .

He's heading for a corner of the courtyard.

KAREN

Where are you going?

TONY

I'm not going back in the house. I'm not dressed for the occasion.

He disappears from view for a moment as Karen moves to the car. Then he reappears, excited.

Karen! Come and have a look at this!

He hauls out an enormous sign and holds it up: 'Kirby, Steele and Oakes, Estate Agents. For Sale.'

He's got it on the market. This is all a front. Bet he's as broke as I am!

EXT. MRS BAGGOT'S PLACE. DAY

Karen and Tony get out of the Renault outside a dusty, old red-brick house, somewhere on the edge of Yeovil. Mrs Baggot, an elderly lady, lean and spry, is feeding chickens.

KAREN

Mrs Baggot?

MRS BAGGOT
(*suspiciously*)

Who's asking?

KAREN

I'm Karen Knowles. And this is Tony Costello. D'you remember us from years ago, with the band?

MRS BAGGOT

Oh, yeah. Beano sold his gold discs, y'know. Well, his wife took everything, the cow. Lives in Wales now. Serve her right.

KAREN

Does he still live with you?

MRS BAGGOT

No, moved away.

KAREN

Where to?

MRS BAGGOT

Over there . . .

She nods in the direction of an old caravan in a field across the road.

. . . He comes home for his meals and his washing.

TONY

D'you know where we could contact him?

MRS BAGGOT

You're the second lot's been looking for him this morning. He's at work. At the nursery.

TONY

He works in a nursery?

KAREN

(*appalled*)

Not with children?

EXT. GARDEN NURSERY. DAY

A large nursery off an A road in Somerset. Beano gets a tray of potted plants for a customer.

BEANO

If you're not going to put these in today, keep them in the shade and give 'em a drink before bedtime. And remember, they don't like lime.

A man and a woman approach. They have solemn Civil Service faces and carry briefcases. Beano sees the couple and the embossed briefcases and senses trouble – but it's too late to run.

TAX MAN

Excuse me. Would you happen to know if Mr David Baggot works here? Sometimes known as 'Beano' Baggot?

BEANO

There was a Mr Baggot worked here a while back. He had to leave. He was allergic to azaleas apparently. Turned his piss green.

TAX WOMAN

Where could we get in touch with him?

BEANO

Not sure. I think one of the girls had a postcard from him. From Zimbabwe.

At that moment a girl shouts from the office.

GIRL

Call for you, Beano!

Beano reacts – that's blown it! He turns away.

BEANO

Be right there, Sarah. Just need to turn the hose off.

Suddenly, he drops the plants and starts to run through the greenhouse, loosening his gardener's apron and tossing it over his shoulder.

TAX WOMAN

Excuse me!

They set off after him.

Beano dodges between rows of potted plants, bags of fertilizer and greenhouses.

HUGHIE

(*voice-over*)

If men are from Mars and women are from Venus, then

drummers are from Pluto. The others were haunted by the past, Beano worried it might catch up with him . . .

Beano runs across a ploughed field, heading for a hedge. He's out of breath, in no shape for this. The two tax officials give chase.

EXT. COUNTRY ROAD. DAY

Beano blunders through the hedge at the rear of the nursery. He staggers into the road and is almost hit by Karen's Renault as it screeches to a halt. He collapses on the hood, panting.

KAREN

Beano!

BEANO

What the fuck are you doing here?

Tony sticks his head out of the passenger window.

TONY

Oi, Beano. How d'you feel about getting the Fruits together again?

Beano reacts with a mixture of astonishment and relief.

BEANO

Not a moment too soon, me old son!

The tax people come through the fence just in time to see the car move away.

INT. LES'S HOUSE. LOFT. DAY

Light falls on a guitar case as a pair of hands pull it from a shelf.

Les's wife, Camille, and their two kids watch from below as Les tinkers with the guitar on the landing. Camille is in her forties, married to Les since she was twenty-two – the only marriage to have survived the Fruits.

Camille shakes her head and ushers the kids away.

INT. RAY'S HOUSE. BEDROOM. DAY

A room with oak panelling and heavy drapes. Ray is in a kimono, trying to find the right remote to turn on the VCR. He stabs angrily at various buttons.

RAY

Bastard! . . . Oh, please, come on, do me a fuckin' favour, would you?

One kicks in the sound system at top volume.

Will you shut up!! Button it!!

He manages to kill the noise. Then another remote opens the drapes, revealing stained-glass windows.

Astrid enters, in a matching kimono.

All I want to do is watch the Brazilian Grand Prix! Which bloody button is it?

ASTRID

There is a limousine outside.

RAY

What?

ASTRID

Obviously Karen do this. She must think we are so easy.

Ray moves to the window.

EXT. RAY'S HOUSE. DRIVEWAY. DAY

A driver stands by a Mercedes limousine. He looks up as Ray's pale face appears in the upstairs window.

DRIVER

Mr Simms? Big fan, sir. The reunion lunch is at twelve-thirty.

RAY

Give me a few minutes . . .

INT. HOTEL MANAGER'S OFFICE. DAY

Kevin hands Karen a fax. She's dressed for the reunion.

KEVIN

This came for you. Try to be back by four, even if it is your last week . . .

Karen scans the fax and the colour drains from her face. She closes her eyes. Then slumps against the wall.

EXT. AVEBURY STONE CIRCLE. DAY

The huge stone circle at Avebury in Wiltshire. Brian and the young Fruits are clowning around for the camera.

EXT. MAIN ROAD. DAY

A helicopter shot shows the limo heading towards the Avebury stones.

INT. LIMOUSINE. DAY

Ray sits in the back, wearing wrap-around shades and a shaggy coat.

RAY

I'm not sure how long this will take.

DRIVER

I'm not booked to take you back, sir. Costello Music said you'd be taking the train.

RAY

Some mistake, surely?

EXT. AVEBURY. PUB. DAY

The limo pulls up outside the timbered pub.

INT. PUB BAR. DAY

The pub is low-beamed, with horse-brasses and a fire in the hearth. Tony and Beano are at the bar, pints in their hands.

BEANO

Weren't you engaged to a Guinness heiress or something?

TONY

Yeah. But they paid me to go away.

BEANO

Not enough by the look of you.

TONY

Never is, mate.

Ray enters, unsure of his welcome.

BEANO

Ray, you old tosser! I was just reminding Tony here about the night in Air Studios we caught you shagging a back-up singer on a Marshall amp.

RAY

Surely not. Why are we meeting here?

TONY

We shot an album cover here years ago.

BEANO

No, that was before Ray's time, wasn't it? . . .

EXT. AVEBURY STONE CIRCLE. DAY

The young Fruits doing a photoshoot at Avebury twenty or so years ago . . .

BEANO

(*voice-over*)

. . . I remember we dropped acid in the Druids' circle . . .

INT. PUB BAR. DAY

BEANO

I remember Brian wrote quite a good song, actually. The last verse even rhymed.

TONY

D'you want a beer, Ray?

RAY

Erm . . . no.

TONY

Jack Daniel's, right?

RAY

Er, no. It's usually Evian nowadays.

(*points to Tony's cigarette*)

. . . and I don't touch those any more.

BEANO

Maybe a sausage then?

RAY

No, I'm on the fourth day of this diet. It's skimmed milk and bananas today.

Tony and Beano shake their heads at how times have changed, as Karen and Les enter the bar.

BEANO

Wey-hey, Wicksie!

Beano gives him a bearhug.

LES

Beano! Tony, nice . . .

Les and Ray eye each other warily before Ray offers a guarded handshake.

So how are you then, Ray?

RAY

Cool, thanks, Les, cool.

Les registers his black T-shirt with a Japanese inscription.

LES

Like the T-shirt. What's that mean, then?

RAY

This? It's a Zen quotation.

BEANO

I thought it was Japanese for Calvin Klein.

RAY

Are we going to get a table or are we waiting for Brian?

KAREN

(*flatly*)

He won't be here . . .

They all stare at her.

. . . I've got news about Brian. See, I reckoned his song royalties must be paid somewhere, so I tried his music publishers. I got a fax just before I left work. It was too late to call you all.

TONY

Call us all about what?

KAREN

All his royalties have been paid direct to a cancer foundation in the States . . . for the last five years.

RAY

He gave his royalties away?

BEANO

He gave his Rolls away once. To his windowcleaner.

KAREN

This is a bequest. Like something you leave in a will.

There's a stunned silence for a moment.

BEANO

You mean the silly sod's dead?

She nods, trying to keep her emotions in check. Everyone just stares at their drinks.

EXT. AVEBURY STONE CIRCLE. DAY

Close on the young Brian, with the others behind him, fooling around for the camera.

EXT. PUB GARDEN. DAY

The whole group has drifted into the garden. It's filled with families on summer days – this isn't one of them. It's cold and dank, with a hint of rain in the air. The mood is more like a wake than a reunion. They walk towards the ancient stones.

RAY

It was always on the cards, something like this. He was . . . y'know what I'm saying. Fragile.

TONY

Yeah, and we crushed him. Keith screwed himself. We screwed up Brian.

Karen can sense the disappointment beneath their sadness.

KAREN

So make it up to him. Do the gig and let people hear his songs. And if Wisbech works out, maybe the record company will re-release some of the old albums.

Tony's the first to leap on this.

TONY

Definitely! What d'you say, lads?

RAY

Can't see it.

LES

Yeah, we'd bollocks it all over again.

Ray reacts – is this a dig at him?

BEANO

Pretty pointless reunion. S'pose I might get a shepherd's pie out of it.

A sound makes them turn. Rock music drifts through the damp air. For a moment no one can tell where it's coming from.

TONY

That's Brian!

LES

Tequila Mockingbird.

TONY

Track one.

A moment later a flock of sheep comes into view over the grassy mound. A young shepherd follows, carrying a boom-box on his shoulder. The guys are amazed.

BEANO

Is that spooky or what?

TONY

It's a sign! A message from the gods of rock 'n' roll . . .

Aerial shot of them standing by the avebury stone circle.

Dissolve to:

INT. REHEARSAL HALL. DAY

It's a Tabernacle Hall with a balcony, used by Sea Scouts. The walls are covered with their regalia – pennants, oars, photographs of battleships. Lots of nervous energy in the room. Ray is wearing shades. He tries out his voice, singing a phrase of 'Dangerous Thing'. Les is talking on a mobile phone. Beano is setting up equipment. Tony plays blues on the organ.

Ray approaches Beano.

RAY

Not sure of the vibe here. Maybe we should've rented somewhere in the country. Somewhere more cloistered.

BEANO

What's wrong with your place, then, Ray? You got a studio and enough bedrooms.

RAY

(*backtracking*)

Oh, that would've been cool, but we're having the lake drained.

He shrugs – what a drag.

Upstairs, Astrid walks from the tiny kitchen with a tray of herbal tea as Karen tries to make a call on the pay phone.

ASTRID

I'm very surprise you do this, you know. I suppose you hope to see Brian again.

KAREN

I'm doing it for all of us . . . What's wrong with this phone?!

ASTRID

Even though you marry, Brian was the love of your life. I think that very sad for a woman of your age.

Karen can't believe she said this. Astrid pushes past her, unaware that she might have caused offence.

HUGHIE

(*voice-over*)

Astrid was wrong. Age isn't sad if you don't give in to it. And if these guys were putting their balls on the block one more time, I was there for them!

Karen reacts to a voice below and moves to the edge of the balcony.

Below her Hughie enters in person, pushing a trolley with equipment on it, a couple of other roadies behind him.

HUGHIE

Fuck me, I canna believe it! What've I strayed into here, *The Night of the Living Dead*?!

The guys respond with delight. Tony plays a triumphant chord on the organ.

BEANO

Hughie, great!

HUGHIE

Jesus Christ, you big sack o'shite, Beano Baggot!

He gives him a bear hug. Tony is next in line.

Tony boy! Look at you!

(*another hug*)

Cuban heels! Look, he's been walking downhill since 1969!

Astrid enters with a tray of tea.

ASTRID

I have made herb tea for everyone! And also dried fruit. You will all get fat if you yust eat Mars Bars.

HUGHIE

Oh, well, Astrid, my wee Nordic charmer! So you and Ray went the distance?

She gives him a Baltic smile and moves away.

BEANO

Still a road-dog, Hughie?

HUGHIE

No. The last tour I did was ten years ago. I did it with Aerosmith, but they'd cleaned up their act. It was all wheat grass juice an' fuckin' pumpkin seeds. I hope you guys are still crazy or I'm oot of here! Hey, wait, I've a wee surprise for you . . .

He beats a tattoo on the huge chest in front of him, covered in stickers from different cities.

Strange Fruit! Rock musicians, poets, legends . . . This is Your Life!!!

He flings the chest open and finds a pair of knickers on top.

Except for these – they're my life.

He pockets them. The guys crowd round, searching through the contents from some long-forgotten tour.

LES

I don't believe it . . . Oh, hello . . .

He pulls out a collection of plaster-cast phalluses.

How did these get in here?

TONY

Groupies usually keep them on their mantelpiece. They sent ours back!

Beano pulls out the biggest, with a distinctive curve in it.

BEANO

Look at this bugger!

(*he taps it like a mike*)

. . . Testing, testing, one, two, three! Ray, ask Astrid if she recognizes this one.

Ray gives a pained reaction. Hughie picks up two of them and turns them into horns on either side of his head. He gives a moose's mating call to Karen, who is looking down on them from the balcony.

HUGHIE

Hey, Karen. A-whooo-ah!! A whoooooh-ah!!!

EXT. REHEARSAL HALL. DAY

Clare arrives with a couple of plastic carrier bags. She can hear the band from outside the hall.

INT. REHEARSAL HALL. DAY

Clare enters and makes a face – it's not her thing. The band are playing 'All Those Dangerous Things'. Ray's attempting to sing and play guitar at the same time. He's having trouble with both, trying to hide his discomfort in a cool front of minimalism.

RAY

'Watch where you turn – it might be today!'

Hughie is at the mixing board. Karen is listening with Astrid.

'You lose your head and then throw it away-hey-yey . . .'

Les clearly doesn't like Ray's performance, making faces to Beano and Tony.

'The wolf's at the door,
The bell starts to ring . . .
I cannot be sure, if it's really him . . .'

Les stops playing.

LES

That's not it!

The others come to a ragged stop. Ray looks at Les.

That's not it.

RAY

What's not *it*?

LES

They way you're singin' it.

RAY

Sorry, Les, it's not a wimpy song, y'know. It's gotta be sung with balls.

LES

Given, Ray, but they can't be borrowed balls, recycled balls. They've gotta be Fruit balls!

BEANO

(*interceding*)

What he's saying is Keith always sang this one with a bit more . . . I dunno, panache.

RAY

You wouldn't know panache if it bit you on the arse, Beano.

Beano does a flamboyant drum break and hits the high hat behind his back. Ray swallows a handful of tiny black pills.

BEANO

Pill break! C'mon, pass 'em round.

RAY

They're from my Chinese herbalist. They won't get you high.

BEANO

Well, we can try!

Tony tries to mediate, walking across to have a tactful word with Ray.

TONY

Ray, look, why don't I take the guitar break on the synth, so you can focus on the singing?

RAY

Well, it would help if I could hear myself above Beano's drumming. He sounds like he's building a shed.

BEANO

Steady!

They watch him walk away.

LES

Maybe he should go back on the sauce, get a bit of juice back in his voice.

Ray hears this – maybe he was meant to.

TONY

Piss off, Les. The guy's easing himself in, we all are.

Hughie's been observing all this.

HUGHIE

In an uncertain world it's good to see that some things never change . . .

INT. JAM RECORDS. LOBBY. DAY

Karen is in the shiny high-tech lobby of Jam Records, somewhere in the West End.

KAREN

These stairs here?

RECEPTIONIST

Straight up.

She passes five young people as she heads up the stairs. They could be a band – they should *be a band. Hip, savvy, street-chic. Their appearance fills Karen with doubt about her own. Why did she pick this suit? And her hair's too neat . . .*

INT. JAM RECORDS. WASHROOM. DAY

Karen's in front of the mirror, changing her image. She undoes another button on her blouse. Then musses up her hair and puts on more eyeshadow.

INT. JAM RECORDS. CLIVE'S OFFICE. DAY

Karen is with Clive Ewing, President of Jam Records, a forty-year-old Australian with close-cropped hair and a discreet diamond in his ear. The office is glass-sided, with the ubiquitous MTV reflected everywhere. A minion stands behind him, a soulful-looking youth who resembles Morrissey but isn't.

CLIVE

So where've you been hiding yourself, Karen?

KAREN

Doing different things. Always wanted to get back into the biz. Just wanted to make sure the timing was right.

CLIVE

Strange Fruit?

KAREN

There's a whole new audience discovering 1970s stuff. This would be a great time to put out some reissues, maybe even a box set.

CLIVE

Whoa! Listen to you, sweetie! Twenty years ago you were Neil Gaydon's doormat.

KAREN

Twenty years ago you were a teaboy at Virgin, Clive. I came to you first.

CLIVE

Only because I own their catalogue.

Karen taps her fingers nervously as Jason, a second minion, enters with coffee.

I used to quite fancy that Brian Lovell. He had that helpless, dirty-sweet Marc Bolan thing. Where is he? Rehab or ashram?

KAREN

We're tracking him down. But the other guys are really juiced.

JASON

Strange Fruit . . . cool name.

CLIVE

Tour them. That's my advice.

KAREN

Good idea. Maybe colleges.

CLIVE

Not the UK, sweetie. Get them across the Channel. See what they've got.

Karen thinks about the wisdom of this.

INT. REHEARSAL HALL. NIGHT

There's more equipment now. Ray is working on a passage of 'All Over the World' with Les and Beano, trying to get it right.

RAY

'All over the world tonight . . .
Feet are hitting the ground . . .'

Tony isn't playing on this one. He's watching from the balcony, standing next to Clare.

TONY

So how d'you feel about your mum getting back into this?

RAY

'Day is following night . . .'

CLARE

Hope we can pay the mortgage next month.

Karen looks up at them curiously from below, wondering what they're talking about.

RAY

'The strong are leading . . .'

TONY

So, tell me, Clare, what's the situation, boyfriend-wise?

CLARE

I've had a couple. Nothing serious.

TONY

I'm talking about your mother.

EXT. REHEARSAL HALL. NIGHT

The music continues inside as Karen takes a break in the night air. Hughie watches her as he lights up a joint.

HUGHIE

Why's a nice wee girl like you putting yourself through all this crap again? Revenge or something?

KAREN

If it's crap, what are you doing here?

HUGHIE

I seem to have this irresistible urge to chronicle human folly.

KAREN

I still love their music. I want to stand in the dark and see an audience feel the way I do.

HUGHIE

Panic-stricken?

Karen laughs and goes over to sit next to him.

KAREN

You know why that is. Because there's a hole in the middle of this band.

HUGHIE

Aye, it's called Brian Lovell. What we need is a guitarist with a bit of charisma . . . Want a wee hit on this?

He offers her his joint.

KAREN

I haven't done that for years.

From inside they hear raised voices and the sound of a cymbal hitting a wall.

HUGHIE

Now might be a very good time to start . . .

INT. REHEARSAL HALL. NIGHT

The guys have stopped playing. Ray moves away from the others, does some yoga stretches and flexes his neck. A pizza guy approaches him with a stack of boxes.

PIZZA GUY

Could you sign this, please?

Ray brightens – famous again. He starts to write as Les and Beano walk over.

RAY

Sure, man. Best wishes to who?

PIZZA GUY

I need a signature for the pizzas.

Ray tries to save face – finishes the signature and walks away. Beano and Les exchange looks.

INT. REHEARSAL HALL. DAY

Close on a guitar. The shot develops to introduce Luke. He's young and cool. And he's good. The others watch, impressed in spite of themselves. Except for Ray and Astrid.

RAY

You sure about this one, Karen?

KAREN

He'll make you sound younger. He'll make you *look* younger.

Luke switches styles with seamless fluency.

ASTRID

This boy is all show-off. We do not need him.

KAREN

Listen. Clive Ewing is paying for these rehearsals and he *might* even underwrite a tour. But sooner or later he's going to notice Brian's not there. So there'd better be someone totally brilliant in his place, right?

ASTRID

Just remember, Karen, Ray is doing this for the boys. We have many other stoves in the fire. We don't need this. C'mon. We are going.

Ray follows her cue and they start to walk out.

KAREN

Tell me, how are Kirby, Steele and Oakes?

ASTRID

I never listen to their music.

KAREN

They're your estate agents! The ones trying to unload Wuthering Heights, so don't tell me you don't need this!

Ray and Astrid react – how did she know this?

ASTRID

You are a bloddy nosy bitch, Karen! Also a slut. I remember Isle of Wight. Come, Ray!

Karen tries to remember what happened in the Isle of Wight as Astrid sweeps off. Ray doesn't follow her. She yells at him in Swedish from the door. He's torn, but still doesn't move.

The guys watch, fascinated, wondering whether Ray will crumble. Astrid yells at him again, still louder as she reaches the door. But he stays. She gives one more furious parting shot and leaves.

Luke has been playing through all this. He looks up now, vaguely aware that something else has been going on.

LUKE

Was that all right?

EXT. LES'S HOUSE. BACK GARDEN. DAY

Les's kids watch from an upstairs window as he says goodbye to Camille.

CAMILLE

Call me.

LES

You know I'll call you. I call you twice a day, even when I'm up a roof. But if this thing works out, you won't see me up a ladder again.

He goes to put his case in the back of a waiting taxi.

CAMILLE

Les, it took us a long time to build this business up.

LES

And I hate it, Camille. I really hate it.

EXT. RAY'S HOUSE. DRIVEWAY. DAY

Another taxi is waiting to take Ray away. Astrid comes to the door with him. Her attitude is one of sullen acceptance. He's wearing a shaggy green fur coat and holding an umbrella against the rain.

ASTRID

Here is your train ticket and your travelling cheques. I have faxed Karen about your vitamins. How many and how often.

Ray just nods. He looks lost and apprehensive, like an evacuee saying goodbye to his mother.

RAY

I wish you were coming with me.

ASTRID

I'm not going on a bloddy boat. Or on a bus with all of them drinking beer and farting. Karen will arrange flights for me. Yust give her your credit card number.

RAY

(*blankly*)

I . . . I don't know my credit card number.

ASTRID

It's on your credit card, Ray.

He nods – 'of course'. She allows him to kiss her cheek. Then he gets into the taxi – without first taking down the umbrella . . .

EXT. REHEARSAL HALL. DAY

A woman in black stands on the cobbled street outside the rehearsal room. She wears a dark tailored suit and black stockings. She watches as a tour bus drives up. In its day it must have looked quite cool, but there are signs of wear and tear.

It pulls up alongside Karen, Clare, Les, Tony, Ray and Luke standing by their luggage. Hughie looks down on them from behind the wheel.

HUGHIE

Feast your eyes on this magnificent land yacht! Tinted windows, air-conditioning, twin portaloos, not to mention an extensive library of pornography, courtesy of the Psychedelic Furs tour of 1988. Step right up!

INT./EXT. TOUR BUS/REHEARSAL HALL. DAY

Everyone starts to climb on board, grateful to get out of the cold. Tony is the first to reach the rear.

TONY

Hey, Hughie!

HUGHIE

Aye.

TONY

Pongs a bit in here. Think one of the Furs is still in here?

HUGHIE

That's pedigree, Tony. Smell that – Dettol, fag-ends, vomit! Yes! I love the smell of vomit in the morning!

EXT. REHEARSAL HALL. DAY

Beano comes into view, carrying a beaten-up bag. The woman in black reacts with interest. Beano notices her. Something about her spooks him. He quickens his pace towards the bus, looking over his shoulder.

WOMAN IN BLACK

Wait!

Beano starts to run. She does too.

Luke reacts to the running footsteps behind him as he enters the bus.

INT./EXT. TOUR BUS/REHEARSAL HALL. DAY

Hughie watches, amused, as he sees Beano running towards them, with the woman in pursuit.

HUGHIE

Karen – look! Harpoon that whale!

EXT. REHEARSAL HALL. DAY

The woman in black loses a shoe. It gives Beano just enough time to elude her, as the guys on board shout encouragement: 'Come on, son!', 'You can do it!' He scrambles aboard, not far ahead of her.

BEANO

Let's get out of here!

INT./EXT. TOUR BUS/REHEARSAL HALL. DAY

Everyone is intrigued, wanting to know the story.

KAREN

Who is she, Beano?

HUGHIE

Paternity suit, is it?

BEANO

Peel rubber, for fuck's sake!

EXT. REHEARSAL HALL. DAY

The woman gives one last despairing bang on the side of the bus with her shoe, yelling 'Wait!' yet again. But it starts to move away.

INT. TOUR BUS. DAY

Beano heads inside, still shaken by the encounter.

BEANO

I bet she's Inland bloody Revenue. That's what happens if you come out of the bloody woodwork.

TONY

What's the problem, man?

BEANO

I owe the buggers thirty-three thousand pounds.

The bus picks up speed as it leaves the car park. The woman is left behind, standing there, catching her breath. Beano slumps into a seat, trying to catch his own.

RAY

Christ, how?!

BEANO

(*irritably*)

Bad management!

RAY

Y'know, Beano, in the history of the Fruits, you're definitely our strongest link to our past.

BEANO

(*pleased*)

Thank you, Ray.

RAY

In all the years I've known you, man, spiritually and emotionally, there's been zero growth. You're what they call a 'flatliner'.

Ray laughs, pleased by his observation. Beano stares at him.

BEANO

Well, it's better than being a wanker!

EXT. DOCKSIDE. DAY

From the bowels of the car ferry, the Strange Fruit bus emerges on to the Ostend docks. The tour is on its way!

INT. TOUR BUS. DAY

Ray joins Karen in the galley area as she finishes a call on her mobile.

RAY

Um, Astrid will want to join us in a couple of days. Could somebody look into flights? Get some options?

KAREN

Sure, Ray . . .

RAY

And when we get to . . . wherever it is we're going . . . I'll need a meeting.

KAREN

A band meeting?

RAY

No. You know . . . AA.

KAREN

No problem.

He moves off.

Luke clowns around into camera. It's for Clare's benefit as she trains her Camcorder on him.

LUKE

So are you enjoying yourself? Doing wardrobe?

CLARE

Trying to get Beano to change his socks – yeah, mad for it.

BEANO

Oi!

LUKE

Didn't you want to come?

CLARE

Didn't have much choice. Mum didn't want to leave me at home. Afraid of what I might get up to.

LUKE

(*brightening*)

Oh, yeah?

EXT. SEAFRONT. DAY

The bus heads north along the coast of Blankenberghe. The place seems shrouded in gloom. Its chalets are boarded up and the sky is as grey as the North Sea which pounds the empty beach.

INT./EXT. TOUR BUS. DAY

Ray sits alone, wrapped in his own insecurities. Beyond him Clare is asleep in Karen's arms, and a card game is in progress – Beano, Les, Tony, Luke and Hughie.

BEANO

America. That was the greatest, wasn't it, Les?

LES

If you say so.

TONY

(*to Luke*)

We toured America on the back of *Sonic Handshake*. That was like our *Sergeant Pepper.* We were mega.

BEANO

(*nostalgically*)

Hollywood Bowl! That was a great gig!

LES

We never played the Hollywood Bowl.

BEANO

Didn't we?

LES

No.

This really shakes Beano.

BEANO

But . . . that's one of my most vivid memories – and it never happened!

The others crack up. Karen sees something outside.

KAREN

I think this is us!

EXT. DUTCH TOWN. DUSK

The bus makes a turn into a narrow side-street. Everyone crowds to the windows to see the venue. Their faces are less than thrilled.

The club is a boat moored on a grimy canal. A billboard outside announces: STRANGE FROOT.

INT. FIRST CLUB. DRESSING ROOM. NIGHT

A minimum of creature comforts. Cracked mirrors, soiled chairs and graffiti on the walls from the bands before them.

Les, Beano, Ray and Luke are half-way through dressing. Tony is heard throwing up in the adjacent toilet. Les, gulping from a bottle of pink liquid, sees Beano's questioning look.

LES

Grumbling ulcer . . .

Ray is putting a brace on his knee.

RAY

Torn cartilage . . .

Beano lets rip an enormous fart.

BEANO

Dutch curry.

The others moan and fan the air. Hughie enters and recoils.

HUGHIE

My God, it's *Night of the Living Dead Two* . . . I'll go and get some of those organ donor cards, I'll be back . . .

He leaves, passing Karen. It's her turn to react, fanning the air.

KAREN

Oh, God . . . where's Tony?

LES

Throwing up.

RAY

This place is a shithole, Karen.

KAREN

It's a happening shithole, Ray.

LES

(*to Beano*)

Someone should tell him we started in places like this.

BEANO

He didn't, he waltzed in when we were fuckin' No. fuckin' 1! When it was all white wine and chicken wings in the dressing room.

RAY

Is that your idea of the high life, Beano, a bottle of warm Blue Nun?

BEANO

Actually, I prefer a very dry Montrachet as a matter of fact . . . Karen, if you spy a couple of toothsome strumps out front, bring 'em round after the gig, will you?

KAREN

Not my job, Beano.

BEANO

Well, it always was!

INT. CLUB. TOILET. NIGHT

Ray's alone. He's staring at himself in the mirror, psyching himself up with quiet intensity.

RAY

You're the man, Ray, you are the man. You are THE man! You are the goddamn motherfucking MAN!! Kick some ass!!! (*he punches his fist and winces at some sudden back pain*) Fuck! . . .

INT. CLUB. NIGHT

The stage is dark, the room noisy. A voice over the PA system in Dutch.

VOICE

Tonight the Waterhole is proud to bring you one of the most famous bands of the 1970s. From England we welcome – Strange Fruit!!

The lights come on to reveal the guys. The audience, heavily punk, react with indifference. The roadies scurry around their feet, connecting leads. Ray steps up to the mike.

RAY

Hello, Belgium!

LES

Holland, you prick!

TONY

Beano!

Beano plays the intro and they start to play. Ray stands with his back to the audience on the tiny stage, arms raised, waiting to turn and face them on cue. He jumps the gun, four bars early, curses and then comes in:

RAY

'I won't get old and change my ways,
The Revolution's now!
Kick out the jams, I want to play,
And don't you bring me down!'

Karen joins Hughie at the mixing board. It's ragged and there's too much reverb, but at least it's rock 'n' roll.

'There's no system in my head,
I can't beat till the day I'm dead . . .'

Tony and Les join in the vocals.

LES/TONY

'Black Moon!'

RAY

'Bright sparks!'

LES/TONY

'Black moon!'

RAY

'So dark!'

LES/TONY

'Black moon!'

RAY

'Well, all right!'

LES/TONY

'Black moon!'

RAY

'It's a black moon night!'

He stumbles back, losing his balance. Les gives him a look darker than any black moon. Beano holds the beat, keeping them in place.

'So people look at me and say
You know some other trip?
The moonlight in the Milky Way
Is in a fuller clip . . .'

Les yells 'One two three' over the lyrics to try and pull them together.

TONY

'Black Moon!'

RAY

'Bright sparks!'

LES/TONY

'Black moon!'

RAY

'So dark!'

LES/TONY

'Black moon!'

RAY

'Well, all right!'

LES/TONY

'Black moon!'

RAY

'It's a black moon night!'

Ray decides to go for the big gesture. He picks up the mike stand and pumps it in the air like Excalibur.

He's forgotten how low the roof is. The stand goes straight through a pipe, showering the stage with water, steam and flakes of rust.

INT. TOUR BUS. NIGHT

Amazingly, the mood is up – good spirits bordering on hysteria. The air is thick with weed, the tables littered with cans of beer. Hughie and Les are playing ukuleles, singing 'Stealing'.

HUGHIE

'I've got me a woman,
Twice my height in size,
She's a married woman,
Comes to see me sometimes.
You don't believe I love,
You don't believe I do . . .'

Tony finds Karen and gives her a warm hug.

TONY

Magic, eh? Doctors, Civil Servants, moguls . . . they've got no idea what it's like. No idea.

HUGHIE

'Stealin' . . . stealin' . . .
Oh, Mama, don't you tell on me . . .'

Karen sees Ray, sitting away from the others, wrapped in his own thoughts. She nods to Tony, who understands and heads down the bus.

'I'm stealin' back to that same old used-to-be . . .'

Tony offers Ray a hit of his joint. Ray shudders – 'no way'.

RAY

I didn't feel like I was happening tonight.

TONY

What you talkin' about?

RAY

I felt I was shouting, not singing.

TONY

Bollocks, you were totally brilliant!

RAY

(*brightening*)

Really?

TONY

Totally. Love you, man.

RAY

I . . . I love you too, Tony.

HUGHIE

'Stealin' . . . stealin' . . .
Oh, Mama, don't you tell on me . . .'

Further up the bus, Beano puts a hand on Luke's shoulder.

BEANO

What did you think, Luke?

LUKE

I thought we were shit, guys.

HUGHIE

'I'm stealin' back to my same old used-to-be . . .'

Les nudges Hughie and he stops playing, suddenly aware of the tension in the air . . .

BEANO

Come again?

LUKE

We were totally crap. I mean, especially on 'Heartbreaker'. Think we should dump that altogether.

TONY

It's a classic.

LUKE

Maybe we should agree what key it's in then.

LES

B flat.

BEANO

C.

Hughie's enjoying this. Karen steps in, trying to head off trouble.

KAREN

Look, the sound was terrible, the stage was too small –

LES

Siddown, Karen. Band stuff.

He turns back to Luke, who realizes he may have overstepped some mark.

Crap?

BEANO

You've got no right in sayin' that, boy.

LUKE

Sorry, man.

LES

We've been round the block, you little shit! We know who we are. Been Fruits a long time.

BEANO

You can't go callin' us 'crap'.

LUKE

Listen, I was out of order –

LES

And we weren't crap. We were seriously, diabolically shite!

Luke hopes they were winding him up but is too scared to ask. Then everybody laughs. Hughie starts to play again and the tension eases. But Ray doesn't get the joke and wonders if this was somehow a dig at him . . .

EXT. HOLLAND. DAY

The bus drives through a dark, forbidding industrial zone. Power pylons and railway sidings. Over we hear the intro to 'Dirty Town'.

INT. SECOND CLUB. NIGHT

The song continues on-stage in another grotty club.

RAY

'The city kills, sucks you dry,
Brings you down, makes you high . . .
Broken glass, broken bones,
Broken dreams and broken homes.
There's no answer when you look around
For some way out of this dirty town.'

While the song continues, Karen argues with the club owner, a forty-year-old greaser in a Harley jacket. He hands her a bundle of dirty notes. She checks them, then runs after him.

KAREN

Hey, clogface! There's more than two hundred people in here. This is not enough.

He says something to her in Dutch.

'Scuse me?

CLUB OWNER

You make me horny. I buy you a drink?

KAREN

Pay me what you owe me and I'll buy *you* a drink, arsehole!

Clare is revealed listening to this. Her jaw drops – this is her mother?

INT. CLUB. TOILET. NIGHT

Tony and Les are at a urinal.

TONY

Almost sounded like a band a couple of times. People are finding their spaces, y'know, man.

LES

Our lead singer isn't. Same old fuckin' poser. Only this time around he hasn't got the chops.

TONY

F'Chrissake, he'll get there.

LES

He should be there! Even if it is just a pisshole in Hoogeven.

TONY

Groningen. We're in a pisshole in Groningen. The Hoogeven pisshole's tomorrow.

Camera reveals Ray's feet under the cubicle door . . .

At the washbasin Tony notices the condom machine.

Oh, yeah, I remember this old model . . .

He gives it two quick slaps on each side and it coughs up a packet of condoms. The door opens and Karen puts her head round the door.

KAREN

We're going for a meal . . .
(*seeing the condoms*)
. . . or do you have other plans?

She closes the door and Tony reacts – how unfair! He hits the machine in frustration – and it delivers another packet.

INT. CLUB. DRESSING ROOM. NIGHT

Karen enters to find only Clare and Luke in the dressing room. He's stripped to the waist and they're sharing a joke.

CLARE

You should be so lucky!

Luke leans in to kiss her.

KAREN

Clare? Clare? Haven't you got washing to collect?

CLARE

(*breaking away*)

Sorry, Mum.

INT. TOUR BUS. NIGHT

The song continues as the bus heads through the night to another gig.

Karen can't sleep. She fingers the sixpence Brian gave her years ago, which she still wears as a charm round her wrist.

Ray wakes with a start, wondering where he is.

INT. THIRD CLUB. TOILET. NIGHT

Ray stares into a cracked mirror, psyching himself up again.

RAY

No problem, man. No problem! Fucking massacre them! Take no prisoners, y'know what I'm saying?

INT. CLUB. NIGHT

'Dirty Town' resumes, in another town, another club.

RAY

'There's no answer when you look around
For some way out of this dirty town,

For some way out of this dirty town.
Dirty town, dirty town . . .'

Surprisingly, in this small manky room, we hear the sound of immense applause and screaming.

INT. AUDITORIUM. BACKSTAGE. NIGHT

But it's not for the Fruits. We're backstage at a big venue. The sound of the band on-stage booms through the walls. The guys are being shot by a TV video unit, making them feel uncomfortable and self-conscious.

The presenter, Zoë Ball, signals for the camera to follow her.

ZOË

Hi, people, Zoë Ball with *Rockpile* here in the Netherlands, where Blind Fish kicked off their European tour. Also present at the gig were rock veterans Strange Fruit. 'All Over the World', yeah!

She moves in on Ray.

Ray Simms, you must be a big follower of the boys?

Ray switches on his interview smile as she thrusts the mike in his face.

RAY

Sure, yeah. I . . . I got on their vibe with their first album.

ZOË

Favourite track?

RAY

(*thrown*)

Oh . . . the third one. Yeah.

Another angle shows the others, looking sourly on.

LES

Why do they always assume that the singer's the voice of the band?

We return to Zoë and Ray.

ZOË

So how do you see your career?

RAY

Well, when I look at my career I feel it's like the universe. It's unfolding on schedule.

Suddenly the camera crew swings off Ray as doors leading from the stage open. Heads turn as a whole platoon of people appear, moving as one. It's Blind Fish, surrounded by roadies and minders in a cocoon of pampered protection – towels, drinks, robes.

Les and the others watch this without enthusiasm.

LES

I don't know what we're doing here.

KAREN

Clive wants it, Les. I mean, the Fish are on his label, we're in the same city, it's a great PR op.

BEANO

How big are these buggers?

LUKE

They're platinum in the States.

BEANO

They don't mean shite in my local.

The stampede sweeps by, past Karen and the rest of the guys, moving through doors, which then slam shut.

LES

Well, that was worth an hour on the fucking autobahn.

The guys shuffle their feet in the cold, cavernous corridor and remember when they *kept people waiting. They look accusingly at Karen – this is dangerous ground.*

KAREN

They need a few minutes, obviously.

BEANO

Well, comrades, the chances of me getting a shag around here are exceedingly slim. I'm off to the bar.

EXT. HOLLAND. DAY

A light dusting of snow is falling as Karen crosses a small canal and enters a building.

INT. COMMUNITY HALL. DAY

A man is on his feet. Dutch speakers will know that he's 'sharing' in a meeting of about fifteen people, men and women of different ages.

Karen slips into the room and takes a seat beside Ray, who's looking very depressed. She keeps her voice low.

KAREN

You OK?

RAY

Oh . . . yeah. I was, y'know, feeling a bit fragile. I needed a meeting. Forgot it would be in Dutch.

KAREN

I blew it last night. I shouldn't have let Clive talk me into it.

RAY

Just seeing them, y'know, *soar* . . . it brought it all back. What we were.

KAREN

What you'll be again.

He shakes his head, doubting this.

RAY

I've got a birthday tomorrow. D'you know how old I'll be?

KAREN

How old?

RAY

Old.

KAREN

You haven't lost it, Ray. You need the big stage, the great arena. That's the kind of artist you are.

She breaks off, realizing that everyone in the room is looking at them. The last speaker is gesturing – it's Ray's turn. Karen squeezes his knee – 'you can do it!' He gets to his feet nervously and clears his throat.

RAY

Um, my name's Ray and um . . . and I'm an alcoholic. And –

There's a puzzled silence, then a large woman looks round.

LARGE WOMAN

Alcoholic?

RAY

Yeah.

LARGE WOMAN

This is Overeaters Anonymous.

Everyone else confirms this. Karen puts her head in her hands. Ray couldn't even find the right meeting! He sits down again.

RAY

Thank you.

EXT. HOLLAND. DAY

The tour bus heads down a long straight road towards a small town.

INT. TOUR BUS. DAY

Hughie is getting exasperated as he tries to explain a game to the others.

HUGHIE

For God's sake, it's easy enough. All you do is name a band whose name corresponds with a part of the body. I'll give you an easy one. The Faces.

RAY

Oh, right.

LES

Small Faces.

HUGHIE

Excellent. That's a point to you.

LUKE

Oh, I've got it . . . Bad Finger!

HUGHIE

Very good.

BEANO

How about Stones? As in kidney stones?

LES

Piss off!

Karen goes into the galley and finds Tony reading on one of the bunks.

KAREN

Find someone to share your condom with, did you?

TONY

No! I merely had that out of professional interest.

KAREN

Run that by me again?

Strange

TONY

That's what I did in Ibiza! All right, it's not something you boast about, but I had the condom concession for the whole of the Balearics. However, I personally am in a profound state of celibacy at the present time.

KAREN

It's of no interest to me, Tony.

TONY

It obviously is. Otherwise, you wouldn't be quizzin' me in that snotty voice of yours.

KAREN

What snotty voice?

TONY

The one you use on club-owners or waitresses.

KAREN

It really doesn't bother me, all right?

Karen walks away, irritated. Tony allows himself a smile – he's getting to her.

All this time the game has continued:

LES

Motorhead!

CLARE

Third Eye Blind.

HUGHIE

Good, good.

RAY

Thumbscrew! First band I was in.

LES

Has to be a band someone's heard of, Ray.

RAY

Bollocks then.

BEANO

You get two points for that.

LUKE

Spooky Tooth.

CLARE

Talking Heads!

HUGHIE

Now we're rolling! Einsteins, every one.

BEANO

Doctor Hook and the Medicine Show!

A collective groan.

CLARE

Objection!

HUGHIE

Objection sustained.

BEANO

Some people have a hook instead of a hand.

LES

It's not a part of the body though, is it? It's not anatomical.

BEANO

It is if you haven't got a fuckin' hand!

EXT. DUTCH TOWN. DAY

It's snowing heavily now, as the bus drives into another Dutch town.

INT. FOURTH CLUB. DAY

This is a couple of rungs up from the other gigs, maybe a converted cinema. Ray is on-stage, working out cues with the local lighting guy.

RAY

Only the footlights at first, ja? Then when the drums kick in, everything up . . .

He sees Hughie on the balcony above, sorting out cables and calls up:

Hughie, I wanna do 'Scream Freedom'. I wanna do it the way we always did, and I want the amps cranked up full volume.

HUGHIE

Full? In this wee place?

RAY

Well, Karen feels I need scale . . .

(*suddenly insecure*)

. . . What do you think?

HUGHIE

Sure, go for it!

(*then, to himself*)

'Scream Freedom'!

INT. TOUR BUS. DAY

Luke and Clare climb quietly on the bus, then react as they see Les, on his own, his back to them, playing acoustic guitar and quietly singing to himself:

LES

'And the flame still burns,
It's there in my soul,
For that unfinished goal.

And the flame still burns
From a glimmer back then
It lights up again in my life.'

They back out, not wanting to interrupt.

EXT. CLUB. REAR ENTRANCE. DAY

They leave the bus and find Hughie unpacking equipment. The sound of Les's singing continues from inside.

LUKE

Good song.

HUGHIE

Oh, yeah. 'The Flame Still Burns'. Les and Brian wrote that after Keith's death.

CLARE

Why don't they play it?

HUGHIE

You're in murky waters there, my dear. See, for a while Les stood in as the lead singer. But he was never a front man. It was obvious to everybody.

LUKE

Is that why he's got it in for Ray?

HUGHIE

The song always meant a great deal to Les, but he hated the way Ray did it. And Ray wouldn't let anyone else do the lead. So they stopped doing it, like, for ever. It's all part of the weird shit that's the history of the Fruits.

LUKE

Be cool to see 'em make it again though.

HUGHIE

We wait with baited breath!

INT. CLUB. DRESSING ROOM. NIGHT

This dressing room is a converted hall, huge and draughty. Beano and Tony are changing and Ray is blow-drying his hair in front of a fly-blown mirror.

BEANO

Sounds a bit grandiose to me. Dry ice in a place like this? I just saw a rat in the bog when I was taking a leak. You don't get that in the Albert Hall.

TONY

Les hates 'Scream Freedom', always did.

RAY

I don't give a flying dog's bollock! I've been doing this for years. I never stopped. He's been whistling up a ladder.

Tony and Beano exchange worried looks as Karen enters.

KAREN

All right, it's full and it's noisy. Lot of head-bangers, lot of skinheads. Rough crowd.

TONY

Maybe we should cut the Joni Mitchell tribute.

RAY

Is there any sign of Astrid?

KAREN

Not yet.

The hair-dryer cuts out. Ray plays with the switch. Nothing. He looks in the mirror. One side of his head is perfectly dry, the other wet strands of hair.

RAY

Fuck!

INT. CLUB. TOILET. NIGHT

Ray is in heavy make-up and a Dracula-like cloak as he psychs himself up in the mirror one more time.

RAY

Tokyo, twenty-three thousand people, Anaheim, forty-four thousand people, Dallas, sixty-seven thousand people – and you give me head-bangers!!!

He screams at himself in the mirror and we cut to:

INT. CLUB. NIGHT

Ray on-stage, screaming at the audience with a demonic howl. His hair looks very strange as he starts to sing.

RAY

'Walking from the gates of Eden
I could hear the sound of freedom
All around!'

Karen looks apprehensive as she watches the band with dry ice swirling around their feet. Les's mood is dark.

'The universe became my cradle
Moons made up my crown . . .'

Beano is worried about something else. Somewhere in the sea of faces is one he's seen before. An older face, in a tailored suit, and she's looking right at him. Christ – is it the woman in black? He ducks beneath the high hat and loses the beat for a moment.

'Now freedom had been found.
Scream freedom!'

Ray gestures to Hughie to turn the volume up. Hughie shakes his head – no.

'Love's in the seventh house.
Scream freedom!'

Ray repeats the gesture. Hughie shrugs – you asked for it – and turns the faders all the way up.

'We heard such pretty sounds
Going round and round . . .'

INSERT: FLASHBACK TO STADIUM

The young Ray singing the same song twenty years ago . . .

RAY

'And round and round . . .'

INT. CLUB. NIGHT

The music is loud. Way too loud. It assaults the audience. Glasses vibrate on the bar and tables jump.

RAY

'Scream freedom!'

EXT. DUTCH TOWN. NIGHT

Quick cuts of the local Dutch populace as their peace is shattered by Strange Fruit's riffs and Ray's hugely amplified voice. Babies cry; dogs bark.

INT. CLUB. NIGHT

A group of skinheads begins to mimic Ray's movements.

Les has had enough of this and kicks the dry-ice machine off the stage. It doubles the amount of smoke, so the band almost disappears completely.

RAY

'Scream freedom!
Love's in the seventh house.
Scream freedom!
We heard such pretty sounds . . .'

The skinheads start to throw everything they can get their hands on. Les strides across the stage towards Ray and yells over the sound of Luke's guitar break.

LES

It's supposed to be rock 'n' roll, man! Not Phantom of the fuckin' Opera!

He strides off-stage. Ray's shoulders slump, the wind knocked out of him. His eyes smart, either from smoke or from emotion. Another missile hits him as he retreats, humiliated, off the stage.

Clare signals to her mother that she's in trouble, surrounded by a bunch of skins, and Karen tries to push towards her.

INT. CLUB. BACKSTAGE. NIGHT

Ray finds Les in the wings, swigging from his antacid bottle.

RAY

I know what you're up to, Les. I've known it since day one. I can feel your eyes in my back every time I go on-stage. Why can't you just get your notes right and remember the lyrics?!

LES

I hate your fucking lyrics!

RAY

Oh, they're not meaningful poetry like Brian's, right?

LES

For him the music was enough. Before the hair and the limos.

RAY

All I remember about Brian is missed cues and missed gigs –

LES

Don't you rubbish Brian!

RAY

And his brother OD'd in a Little Chef and you still worship

the ground he vomited on! It's not 'cause they're great, it's 'cause they're dead! Maybe if I was dead I'd get some respect!

LES

It'd be a start!

He walks off. Ray, stung, is left alone, with nothing but the noises of derision echoing in his ears. Then he sees something.

On a table is an enormous cake. Icing spells out 'HAPPY FIVE-OH, RAY!' *He stares at it. Then picks it up and hurls it against the wall.*

RAY

I'm not fifty!!!

INT. CLUB. NIGHT

Tony sees Karen in trouble with the skins and signals Luke to stop playing.

KAREN

Back off! Back off!

She pushes off the largest of the skins. Tony fights his way towards them. He taps the skin on the shoulder.

TONY

You got a problem, pick on me!

The skin does. He nuts Tony, who staggers back, clutching his nose.

EXT. CLUB. NIGHT

Police cars arrive at the club, sirens blaring.

EXT. CLUB. REAR ENTRANCE. NIGHT

Everyone – except Ray – is lending a hand, running from the club, trying to cram equipment into the tour bus.

KAREN

Where's Ray?

LUKE

No one's seen him, Karen.

LES

He's doing one of his moodies. And don't go chasing after him, 'cause that's what he wants.

BEANO

Hope this isn't another Sunderland.

LUKE

What happened in Sunderland?

BEANO

He tried to slash his wrists with my Swiss Army knife.

LES

He'd never find the right blade.

KAREN

This could be serious. He's on Prozac, Astrid told me.

BEANO

Prozac and alfalfa sprouts, that could be lethal . . .

EXT. HOTEL. NIGHT

The tour bus is parked outside a hotel with a neon beer sign blinking in a downstairs window.

INT. HOTEL BAR. NIGHT

A bleak, awful room with orange vinyl chairs, a couple of 'baby-foot' machines and a pool table. Young girls are clustered around Luke.

LUKE

I love playing the guitar, y'know what I'm sayin'?

Clare can see the way this is going. She slams down her cue on the pool table and walks off angrily.

Beano and Hughie are in the bar.

BEANO

Not much joy here for me tonight. Think I might retire to my boudoir – if the youngsters will keep the noise down a bit.

HUGHIE

Hell's teeth, Beano, you sound like their father.

BEANO

I might be. We toured here twenty years ago. And I know I had a shag then.

Further down the bar tension is simmering between Tony and Les. Tony belts down a shot.

TONY

Y'know what your problem is, man? You see yourself as the keeper of the fuckin' flame. You've got all these reasons for your anger. Ray's style, Ray's taste, Ray's lyrics.

LES

His shoes piss me off an' all.

TONY

You know what the truth is? You had your shot and you couldn't hack it!

Hughie's clocked this. He gives a wicked grin.

HUGHIE

Dear me, trouble in paradise . . .

TONY

(*angrily*)

Fuck off, Hughie! Why'd you come on this ride anyway? Just to watch us bollix it all up again?

HUGHIE

Maybe the antique trade's a bit slow this time of year, eh?

Tony looks as if he wants to whack him. But suddenly Beano's in his face.

BEANO

Blood, Sweat and Tears!

TONY

What?

BEANO

Name of a band, parts of the body – triple whammy, right? Oh, fuck!

He belly-flops to the floor. The others look towards the door to see the reason. The woman in black has entered! Beano whispers hoarsely from the floor:

It's the woman from the tax! I thought I saw her at the gig!

He crabs away under the tables on his hands and knees, taking advantage of the natural cover.

INT. HOTEL LOBBY. NIGHT

Karen comes downstairs, followed by Clare and a policeman.

CLARE

Mum, I want to go home. I'm sick of this.

A bunch of angry Dutch locals are waiting for her at the reception desk, all talking at once.

KAREN

Not now, love. I've got my hands full.

CLARE

But this is stupid. Why don't we just pack it in?

One of the locals shouts at Karen in guttural tones. She turns to the receptionist for translation.

KAREN

What's he saying?

RECEPTIONIST

He wants the police to impound your bus.

Karen can also see Luke necking with one of the girls in a doorway, and Beano, for some reason, hiding under a table.

KAREN

Tell him that Strange Fruit are a well-established phenomenon on the British music scene and will live up to their obligations.

CLARE

Obligations? Why don't you live up to yours and get us out of here?

KAREN

(*nodding towards Luke*)

This isn't about me, is it? It's about *him.*

Clare glares at her mother and storms off.

EXT. DUTCH TOWN. BACKSTREET. NIGHT

Ray comes into view, still wearing his stage make-up and clothes. His breath condenses in the cold night air. A kid comes out of a doorway.

DUTCH KID

Hey, Fruit. Want to get high?

Ray thinks about this. Thinks about all the meetings he's been to, and all the reasons to say no. Then:

RAY

What you got?

DUTCH KID

You want to go up, or you want to go down?

RAY

Oh, down. Definitely down . . .

The kid produces a bag of pills.

EXT. POLICE STATION. NIGHT

Karen leaves the police station to find Tony waiting.

TONY

I heard you were here, love. You OK?

KAREN

Not really, no. They want to hold the bus till I get money wired over for the damages. What made me think I could do this, Tony?

TONY

It's only you who's held us together this long . . .

They start to walk down the street. It's covered in ice and frozen slush. A vehicle approaches slowly ahead of them.

Look, you're gonna need some help. Financial, I mean. I want you to have this.

Karen turns to see he has the locket in his hand.

KAREN

No, no, no. This is your fall-back, this is your rainy day.

TONY

It's yours now.

He opens the locket. The tooth falls to the ground.

Oh, shit . . .

And then they're both on their knees, trying to find it.

Christ, where's the tooth? Oh, shit! Oh, no! Where is it?

He registers the approaching vehicle, spreading grit on the icy road. Alarmed, Tony leaps in front of it.

Hold on, man!

The vehicle shows no sign of stopping.

STOP!!! You're violating a piece of rock 'n' roll history!

Karen grabs Tony's arm and yanks him to safety. The road is showered with grit, each individual piece about the size of a tooth . . .

EXT. TOWPATH. NIGHT

Ray's melancholy figure approaches the bank of a frozen canal.

RAY

'They called him the Prince of Darkness,
And he ruled the Zuyder Zee,
And he only had one mantra . . .
To be . . .'

He fumbles with a plastic bag of pills. Drops them and they 'ping' on the frozen ice.

Oh, bugger me!

He kneels down to retrieve one of the pills from the ice.

Bollocks!

He swallows it. As he stands up, there's a cracking sound beneath him. Ray doesn't recognize it at first – it's not a familiar sound. Then he hears it again.

Oh, fuck . . . Oh, no . . .

EXT. HOTEL. NIGHT

Clare leaves the hotel, wearing a heavy coat, a long woollen scarf and a backpack. She stops as she hears a familiar voice.

RAY

(*voice-over*)

Somebody!!

Clare starts to run.

EXT. FROZEN CANAL. NIGHT

Clare comes into view and sees Ray stranded on the ice.

CLARE

Ray?

Ray looks up in relief to see Clare.

RAY

Clare? Thank God!

He gasps in relief. Without warning, the ice gives way beneath him and he disappears into the inky-black water!

CLARE

Oh, my God!! Ray? Ray? Somebody!!!

UNDERWATER: CANAL. NIGHT

In slow motion we follow Ray, plunging into a surreal netherworld. Surprisingly, there's no panic on his face, just a faint smile, as if he's seen something quite lovely. His eyes close, as if he's succumbing to Sweet Sister Death. For a moment he sees young Brian, floating in the water with him.

His face is briefly visible beneath a patch of ice, then disappears again . . .

EXT. FROZEN CANAL. NIGHT

Clare is still shouting for anybody to come and help her. Nobody answers. The evening is still, silent.

Then, suddenly, Ray's boot with three-inch heels comes through the ice! Clare reacts in relief. A moment later his head breaks the surface.

Clare rushes to the edge of the towpath.

CLARE

Ray, for God's sake! Grab this!

She tosses him one end of her scarf and he gets hold of it. She hauls him to the bank, more ice cracking around him. Then she grabs his coat collar and hauls him on to the towpath. She wraps her arms around him as they both try to catch their breath.

RAY

I think I had a near-death experience.

CLARE

It was almost a full-death experience.

RAY

I slipped, Clare.

CLARE

You're on a frozen canal, Ray.

She helps him up. He has to hold on to her for support.

RAY

The tragedy for people like me is our lives peak too early.

CLARE

Tragedy? Famine's a tragedy, Ray. Or knocking down the rainforests. Anyway, some people's lives never peak, ever. Think about it

She supports him as they move away.

Happy birthday, by the way.

RAY

I'm not fifty!

EXT. SIDE-STREET. NIGHT

Karen and Tony are still where we left them, in the snowy street.

TONY

Aw, bollocks! Maybe the tooth fairy will find it.

Close on them as they give up the search and stand up.

KAREN

Y'know, that was the nicest thing anyone's ever done for me.

TONY

(*suddenly serious*)

I'd do anything for you, you know that. If you weren't so hung up on Brian, I'd've married you years ago. I told you once. Remember? In Detroit?

KAREN

No, it was Cardiff.

TONY

Close.

He moves in to kiss her. She pushes him gently away.

KAREN

Brian . . .

Tony freezes. The moment is shattered. Karen instantly realizes her mistake.

Tony . . . let's get back to the hotel.

She starts to walk down the road. He hesitates.

TONY

Karen?

She turns.

Why are you still chasing ghosts?

She doesn't know the answer yet.

INT. HOTEL LOBBY. NIGHT

Astrid is walking up the stairs when Karen enters the hotel. She sees Astrid and hopes to avoid her. Too late!

ASTRID

Karen! I am at Amsterdam at three o'clock. There is no limousine. I wait an hour. I not know who to call. You give no number. I get train to this terrible place, then the taxi driver, he is a fool, he has not heard about the club. He has not heard about the hotel! I have to tell you I am very bloddy pissed off!!

Before Karen can respond, Clare comes in from the street, still supporting Ray. The pills have kicked in and he's finding it hard to keep his eyes open.

Astrid is shocked and distressed to see him in this condition. But he's blissfully unaware of it, thrilled to see her.

RAY

Hello, baby . . .

(*to Clare*)

I'm all right now, thank you. Whass happenin'?

ASTRID

What happened to you?

He stumbles up the stairs towards her.

RAY

I love you, Momma!

He sinks to his knees, blissfully 'luded, his head in her belly . . .

INT. HOTEL BEDROOM. NIGHT

The digital reads 4:10. Sounds of passion from figures beneath the bedclothes. The telephone rings.

It's Hughie's face that appears from under the sheets. He grabs the receiver. Can't believe there's another problem.

HUGHIE

What?!

We can't identify the voice at the other end.

VOICE

Cockney Rebel . . . 'Cock' and 'Knee'. Bonus points for that one, surely?

A laugh and the phone goes dead.

HUGHIE

Bastard!

He returns to the joys of his wee guest. After a few more seconds, the phone rings again. Hughie reaches for it, really pissed off now.

Who the fuck is this?! . . .

KAREN

(*voice-over*)

It's me, Hughie.

HUGHIE

Oh, sorry, boss. I mean, Karen.

KAREN

(*voice-over*)

Get your socks on, mate. We're leaving.

HUGHIE

What, now?! . . .

EXT. HOTEL CAR PARK. NIGHT

It's still pre-dawn as the band file furtively and swiftly from the hotel, some still pulling on their clothes, rubbing sleep from their eyes. Karen is at the door of the bus, hurrying them along, urging everyone to be quiet.

Tony is the last to scramble on board. Hughie starts the engine, revs up and crunches the gears horribly.

The bus accelerates, demolishing part of a chain-link fence, knocking over rubbish bins. Then it joins the main road, free and clear!

INT. TOUR BUS. DAY

Beano has a copy of Mojo *magazine with a full-page picture of Jimi Hendrix. He finishes blacking out a tooth, then shows the page to Tony.*

BEANO

Here – was this your tooth, Tone?

TONY

Hilarious, Beano.

BEANO

Arf, arf!

Les knocks tentatively on one of the bunks. The curtains are pulled back to reveal Ray and Astrid. She's giving Ray a face massage.

LES

About last night, Ray . . . I mean, it's a heavy thought that I drove you to do something that desperate.

RAY

What? Oh, well, y'know, man. Dark night of the soul, I suppose.

LES

Yeah, well. There's maybe some things I shouldn't have said. Shouldn't have said them twenty years ago, probably.

ASTRID

He says he's a very bastard pig, Ray.

Karen and Tony are observing this exchange.

KAREN

Does Les think Ray was trying to kill himself, Tony?

TONY

I may have given him that impression, yes.

(*he looks at her*)

. . . Best for the band, I thought.

Les turns away. He's said as much as he's able to. But Ray grabs his arm.

RAY

Les, you should know this. Last night, as the icy waters closed over me, I saw Brian.

Les doesn't quite know how to respond.

LES

What was he wearing.

RAY

(*thrown*)

What? I don't remember. But I saw him so clearly. Maybe he was on some astral travel trip, I don't know . . .

He leans in and whispers, to give his words emphasis.

But he was sending a message. And the message was positive, man!

Les nods. As he straightens up, he notices Hughie and Luke, listening to this exchange from the upper bunks. He glares at them and moves off.

The bus backfires and judders to a halt.

EXT. ROADSIDE LAY-BY. DAY

The bus has broken down. The roadies have got their heads under the hood. Everyone else is outside, getting some air or kicking a ball around.

Karen watches the others for a moment. Lack of sleep and strain have taken their toll. There are shadows under her eyes and she hasn't bothered to put on any make-up.

KAREN

I'd better call the club. Tell them we might not make the gig.

There are a few coughs and half-averted eyes.

BEANO

Well, the fates do seem to have conspired against us. What's that quaint old-fashioned Scottish proverb, Hughie? 'If at first you don't succeed . . .'

HUGHIE

(*gravely*)

'Pull your foreskin over your heed.'

KAREN

(*angrily*)

Is that how you all feel? Is it? 'Cause if it is I'd like to know and we can all piss off home and get on with the rest of our lives!

No one answers. Karen turns her back on them all, frustrated and angry.

Two young hitchhikers approach, pretty girls in parkas and backpacks. One of them speaks faltering English.

HITCHHIKER

Excuse. You go maybe to Antwerp?

Beano is the first to respond, turning on the charm.

BEANO

Hasn't been decided yet, my lovely.

Les is the first to see it. She's wearing an old T-shirt with the words 'Strange Fruit – World Tour, '77' on the front.

LES

Hey – where d'you get that T-shirt?

HITCHHIKER

This? It belong my father.

She opens up the jacket so they can all see it clearly.

BEANO

Look at that . . .

TONY

'77 . . . Must've been through the wash a few times.

HITCHHIKER

My father, he die.

They all make sympathetic mumbles.

LES

That's a shitter.

HITCHHIKER

They were his favourite band. He say, best band he ever saw.

She stands there, shivering, not realizing how she's warmed their hearts. The guys stare at her, then at each other.

TONY

It's another sign . . .

RAY

(*emphatically*)

Brian sent her!

And suddenly, behind them, the engine splutters into life.

INT. ANTWERP. CLUB. NIGHT

The band start to play. Something has happened to them. Maybe it's all the events they've been through, maybe it was the hitchhiker. But there's an attitude, a unity, that's tangible. Ray grabs the mike.

RAY

'All over the world tonight,
Feet are hitting the ground!
And day is following night.

The strong are leading!
All over the world tonight,
Clocks are spinnin' around!
They're putting the world to right.
The weak are dreaming!
Crossing the border of innocence,
We're breaking down the walls of time.
All over the world, it's happening,
It's happening tonight.'

The others join him for the hook.

ALL

'All over the world!
All over the world!'

RAY

'We'll slay the dragon, it has to happen.
Love is making, the future's breaking,
All over the world – tonight!'

Somehow the two pretty hitchhikers have ended up beside Hughie and he's showing them how the mixer works.

Jason and Not-Morrissey arrive. They reach Karen, tap her on the shoulder and mouth 'Hi's.

'All over the world tonight,
Love is always the verb . . .'

JASON

Band sound good!

RAY

'And now the heat is on . . .'

KAREN

Wicked!

RAY

'With this frustration!'

Astrid's transfixed, switching from nursemaid to groupie, suddenly the teenage fan she was all those years ago in Sweden. She starts to bop around, hair loosening, hips swivelling.

'All over the world!
All over the world!
We'll slay the dragon, it has to happen.
Love is making, my future's breaking . . .'

Astrid frowns, seeing that young girls at the foot of the stage are turned on too.

'All over the world!
All over the world tonight,
And leave by satellite.
Crossing the borders of innocence,
We're breaking down the walls of time.'

Astrid pushes forward, elbowing the girls aside, hitting one of them across the head with her Prada purse.

ASTRID

Back off, you sluts, he's mine!!

Then she jumps on stage and gives Ray a quick kiss on the cheek.

RAY

'All over the world tonight,
All over the world tonight,
We'll slay the dragon, it has to happen.
Love is making, the future's breaking,
All over the world – tonight!
We're all right! Tonight!'

The band get the biggest roar they've heard in years. And the looks that pass between them say they know they deserve it.

EXT. OSTEND. DOCKS. DAY

The cheers continue as the tour bus drives on to the ferry taking them back to Britain.

HUGHIE

(*voice-over*)

A week later they had a record deal. Straight into the studio and Ray let Les sing! Just the one song, mind, but on a scale of miracles this rated about level with the Immaculate Conception.

INT. RECORDING STUDIO. NIGHT

The studio is a converted church with high ceilings and ecclesiastical features. Big enough for a concert grand, a motorbike, a suit of armour, a bed and a ping-pong table.

Les is singing a ballad to playback.

LES

'. . . Always standing in the same old lines,
Moving sideways to the march of time.
What might have been,
What might have been,
A portrait of my life.
No fool would say, you live today
Without a will to survive . . .'

Ray nods supportively from the booth, digging the song.

INT. RECORDING STUDIO. NIGHT

Later on, Beano and Les are playing table tennis. Karen's voice comes over the talkback.

KAREN

Zoë Ball's programme is on, guys.

BEANO

In a minute. Money on this . . .

He serves.

INT. RECORDING STUDIO BOOTH. NIGHT

Karen, Tony, Ray, Hughie and Luke sit round the TV.

On-screen, Zoë Ball sits on a stool with TV monitors behind her, doing the link to the next segment of her late-night rock programme.

ZOË

(*off-screen*)

. . . And in Holland I also caught up with seminal 1970s rockers, Strange Fruit . . .

The style of the piece is very modish – quick cuts, jump cuts, strange angles and fast zooms. The guys cheer when they see themselves on screen.

(*to Ray*)

So why do you guys play such down-and-out venues?

RAY

(*off-screen*)

This tour we wanted to be more grass roots, y'know? Like, with the audience right in your face!

ZOË

(*off-screen*)

So as a band, do you miss Brian?

Beano and Les appear on screen, both looking the worse for wear.

LES

(*off-screen*)

Well, if you want my opinion Brian Lovell was as near to a genius as you can get in this business –

KAREN

I don't remember this.

LUKE

You'd left. She got them tanked up in the Green Room.

The others shush them as they listen to the words on screen.

LES

(*off-screen*)

See, people who remember the Fruits remember Keith and Brian.

BEANO

(*off-screen*)

Yeah, they don't remember Wicksey, they don't remember Ray, don't remember me! 'Cept maybe when I fell off the stage at Glastonbury once, pissed as a bollock.

He swigs his drink and wipes his mouth with the back of his hand. In the room no one knows where to look. Karen reacts – 'Oh, God, there's more.' Ray glares through the glass at Les and Beano, still playing table tennis.

Ain't no fuckin' use kidding yourself we're Strange Fruit, 'cause we ain't. Not with Keith and Brian ten feet under.

TONY

You dickhead, Beano!

BEANO

Maybe if we was to call ourselves 'Slightly Strange Fruit' . . .

LES

Or how's about 'Fairly Ordinary Fruit' . . .

BEANO

Yeah, or 'Canned Fruit'? . . . I'm canned, don't know about you!

On-screen Beano belches and gives a lopsided grin. Ray suddenly jumps up and runs out of the room.

KAREN

Ray!

She and the others follow him.

INT. RECORDING STUDIO. NIGHT

Beano and Les are in full flight at the ping-pong table as Ray bursts in.

RAY

You fuckin' arseholes!

BEANO

Hang about, Ray, set point.

He serves. Ray seizes the table and tips it over, just as Karen and the others come through the door.

What's rattled your eyeliner, then?

RAY

You two just crapped all over this band!

Ray shoves Beano. He tumbles backwards. Ray dives on top of him. Les tries to pull him off.

LES

Thats enough, man!

RAY

Get off me!

LES

That's enough!!

Beano turns towards Ray, pointing to a peculiar bulge in his cheek. Ray is suddenly contrite.

RAY

God, I'm so sorry, Beano –

Beano exhales. A ping-pong ball flies out of his mouth and hits Ray in the eye!

The fight is on again. Ray charges Beano, drilling his head into his chest. They collide with the suit of armour. It crashes to the floor. Hughie and Tony try to break them up.

HUGHIE

Let it go! You'll be hitting each other with your handbags next!

Ray moves aside, still steaming. He turns on all of them.

RAY

You guys never forgave me for taking over from Keith. Ever. Well, you can find yourself another fucking singer!

He walks out. Suddenly all Tony's frustrations and anxieties explode.

TONY

F'Chrissake, this was about *us*! This was our second shot and it was working! Anyone who was at Antwerp saw that. We were fucking brilliant. We were better than we ever were. We were a great band.

No one knows where to look or what to say.

You stupid bastards! Why couldn't you bury the past before it buried us?

Les singing 'What Might Have Been' continues over the following images:

EXT. SOUTH LONDON. COUNCIL FLATS. NIGHT

Karen's Renault is parked outside the dark hulk of a council tower block. Tony is beside her in the car, still numb from what's happened.

He unclips his seat belt and gets out. She watches him walk under the sodium streetlights towards the graffiti-scarred building.

Dissolve to:

EXT. RAY'S HOUSE. FRONT GATES. DAY

Ray and a workman carry the 'For Sale' sign through the front gates of his Gothic pile.

Dissolve to:

EXT. ROOFTOP. DAY

Les is in his work clothes, carrying his tools, back on a roof on a sunless day. There's a blank, flat look on his face.

Dissolve to:

EXT. CEMETERY. DAY

Karen and Clare walk between headstones, both carrying a small bunch of flowers. The music fades.

HUGHIE
(*voice-over*)
Ironically, a week later was the twenty-fifth anniversary of Keith's death. Maybe because she didn't have a grave for Brian, Karen went to pay her respects.

They reach a tombstone where several floral tributes have been laid. Karen kneels down and puts their flowers with the others. Clare looks at some of the cards.

CLARE
God, look at them all . . . This one's written in Dutch . . .
(*she reads another*)
'Even after all this time . . . the Flame Still Burns. Love you, man . . . Brian.'

Karen stares at her daughter, then checks the card, her mind reeling.

EXT. CAMDEN MARKET. DAY

Karen and Clare face Hughie as he dismantles his stall.

KAREN

Where is he, Hughie? He's alive, isn't he?

Hughie says nothing, shoving boxes into the back of his van.

We went to the cemetery. He'd sent flowers to his brother!

HUGHIE

Probably some crazy fan with a twisted sense of humour.

KAREN

Or it could've been you, Hughie. Looking after him like you always did.

He stops what he's doing, avoiding her eye. And Karen knows she's right.

I thought he was dead! Why did you put me through that?

HUGHIE

Because I love the wee guy.

KAREN

You're not the only one!

HUGHIE

Look, when he came back from the States a few years ago he was a right basket case. I couldn't risk letting him mix with the other guys. Putting him through all that shit again.

KAREN

Maybe it wouldn't have been 'all that shit again' if he'd been with them!

HUGHIE

But it was, wasn't it? People don't change. There's no blinding flash on the road to Damascus.

KAREN

Listen, Hughie, the guys don't deserve this. You saw how close they were. You were there.

CLARE

Did you tell him? How good they were?

HUGHIE

As a matter of fact I did. Even played him a couple of tracks . . .

EXT. HOSPITAL. DAY

Karen and Tony walk with a uniformed nurse through the grounds of an institutional building. She points ahead and they thank her, walking past several patients. Tony is uncomfortable; he doesn't like hospitals.

TONY

Maybe you should talk to him first.

Karen nods and he hangs back as she continues walking.

EXT. HOSPITAL GARDEN. DAY

Further on is a complete surprise. A miniature Japanese garden has been created, complete with bonsai trees, landscaped flower borders and ornamental stones.

Karen rounds a corner and sees a figure in a long black overcoat kneeling on the ground. After a moment he turns, as if sensing her presence.

Even at a distance Karen recognizes Brian. He has the same wiry body and boyish face. Just a little grey in the long, untidy hair. He removes his shades as she approaches. They stare at each other for a long moment.

BRIAN

I was trying to picture what you'd be like. Still look like yourself.

KAREN

You don't look much different. A few more lines. Less than you deserve. So how long have you been working here?

BRIAN

Since I stopped being a patient. Kind of handy, if I have a relapse.

KAREN

But you're fine now?

BRIAN

Did you know Tchaikovsky, when he was conducting, used to cradle a hand on his head because he thought it might fall off? Did you know that?

KAREN

I didn't know that, no. Is that how you felt? Is that why you gave your royalties away, you silly sod?

BRIAN

No. The only way I could get away from the life I had was to start again with a new one. D'you like my garden?

KAREN

It's beautiful.

BRIAN

I write songs in here. I've got over a hundred of 'em in a Sainsbury's plastic bag.

KAREN

So did you play the tracks, the Fruits' tracks?

BRIAN

Yeah. A little too much reverb for my taste. But they were definitely happening.

KAREN

They missed you.

BRIAN

I miss them.

KAREN

Is there anything in the rules says I can't give you a hug?

BRIAN

Not that I know of.

Karen steps tentatively forward and wraps her arms round him.

Tony enters the garden and sees their embrace. He wonders where this leaves him and turns away.

Karen and Brian break apart, a little awkward with each other.

So why did you leave me, all those years ago?

KAREN

I didn't want to watch you die . . .

EXT. HOSPITAL FRONT ENTRANCE. DAY

Karen and Tony walk towards her car. Tears are rolling down her face and her shoulders shake as the sobs become deeper. He takes her hand, trying to give her comfort. But he says nothing, trying to let her work out her own emotions.

Dissolve to:

EXT. RAY'S HOUSE. DAY

A wide shot of Ray's house – wide enough to see the holes in the roof. We hear Astrid giving a sales pitch:

ASTRID

(*voice-over*)

The house has much history. Queen Victoria slept here, and so did Stevie Winwood . . .

INT. RAY'S HOUSE. STUDIO. DAY

Astrid excuses herself from the prospective buyers as the phone rings.

ASTRID

Excuse me . . . Yes?

KAREN

(*off-screen*)

Hello, Astrid, it's Karen. Is Ray there?

Astrid's cheeks flush with anger.

ASTRID

No, you cannot see Ray!

EXT. RAY'S HOUSE. FRONT GATES. DAY

Karen is with Tony by her Renault at the intercom.

ASTRID

(*voice-over*)

He never wish to see any of you bloddy people again!

The voice clicks off. Karen reacts in frustration. Brian steps forward.

BRIAN

He'll see me . . .

He starts to climb over the ornamental wrought-iron gates.

KAREN

Brian, careful . . .

EXT. RAY'S HOUSE. GROUNDS. DAY

Ray sits in the lotus position, his back to a massive tree, facing a small lake. He wears an old afghan coat, a relic from the 1960s. He's meditating, eyes closed, his voice intoning a long 'Ommmmmm'. He breaks off and opens his eyes. They widen in amazement.

What he sees is Brian, standing by the edge of the water. An apparition that he's somehow conjured from the past.

Ray closes his eyes tighter and resumes his 'Omm', a semitone higher. Opens them to see Brian, a little nearer now. He closes them again and 'Omm's with even more intensity.

When he opens his eyes this time Brian is peering into his face. Ray's voice is a whisper.

RAY

I can see you, Brian. So clearly! D'you have a message?

BRIAN

We've got a gig on Saturday, man!

Ray is totally confused.

EXT. WISBECH FESTIVAL. DAY

A helicopter shot shows the setting sun and a crowd of thousands gathered to hear the music. Over a voice:

REPORTER

There seems to be a record number of people down there. Maybe two hundred thousand. Wisbech is happening!

EXT. VIP ENCLOSURE. DAY

Steve Greenblatt comes forward to greet the Fruits as they emerge from their limos. He sees Tony first – the guy who began it all.

STEVE

Tony!

TONY

How are you, man?

STEVE

Great to see you! Guys, this is a great thrill for me! Brian Lovell! Listen, I'm really pleased the rumours of your demise were a little premature.

Brian nods, but he's not really listening. He's looking around him apprehensively. Hughie ushers him along.

TONY

I hope we're going on after Mott the Hoople this time.

STEVEN

Yeah, after Mott, and Little Feat.

BEANO

Little *Feat* – one point!

INT. VIP TENT. NIGHT

A small area has been cordoned off for the media, a rectangle of Astroturf and a circle of uncomfortable chairs. It's Strange Fruit's turn and they face several camera crews and reporters. The tone of the questions is irreverent and facetious.

SNOTTY REPORTER

So which Fruit's which then?

BEANO

Well, I'm Posh Fruit, Les is Sour Fruit, Ray's the only one that's got any money so I suppose he's Bread Fruit.

ZOË

What's that make you, Brian? Bruised Fruit?

Most of them laugh. Brian doesn't. He looks perplexed and a little panicked.

Beano sees something to panic him – the woman in black is standing behind the press! She's in her usual tailored suit, with the incongruous addition of a backstage pass on the lapel. She gives him a little wave.

Beano gets to his feet and tries to find a way out through the flaps of the tent.

Meanwhile:

FIRST REPORTER

Brian, twenty years ago in the *Melody Maker* you said, and I quote, 'I will never walk on-stage with the Fruits again.' How'd you feel about that now?

Les answers for him.

LES

Since when did anyone believe what they read in the *Melody Maker*?

Beano re-emerges to find he's still inside the tent! The woman is still looking at him knowingly. He backtracks and manages to scramble away.

SECOND REPORTER

Did you try any new material on the tour or was it just Golden Oldies?

SNOTTY REPORTER

Any punch-ups on the tour? There always used to be.

TONY

No, it was all sweetness and light.

RAY

Very mellow vibe.

EXT. BACKSTAGE. NIGHT

Beano emerges from the tent, stumbling backwards over guy ropes, to find himself in the open air. He gives a deep sigh of relief.

But, suddenly, there she is, twenty yards away, standing in a pool of light at the end of a row of vehicles.

BEANO

Oh, fuck!

He ducks beneath the tow bar of a trailer and disappears.

INT. VIP TENT. NIGHT

The press conference continues.

FEMALE REPORTER

Did you guys plant this story about Brian's death? I mean, was the whole thing a publicity stunt?

LES

(*irritated*)

Of course it wasn't.

The questions come faster, overlapping, all directed at Brian.

FIRST REPORTER

There have been question about your life, Brian –

SECOND REPORTER

What have you been doing?

THIRD REPORTER

Was the pressure too much the first time around?

FEMALE REPORTER

Wasn't that the reason you lost the plot in the first place?

Brian looks bewildered, blinking as the flashbulbs pop. Karen and the boys are starting to worry about him.

MEDIATOR

One question at a time, please.

ZOË

Brian, were you really in a mental home?

SECOND REPORTER

Were you in a clinic?

FIRST REPORTER

What caused your crack-up?

FOURTH REPORTER

Are you a recluse?

SNOTTY REPORTER

Was your breakdown chemically induced or was it brought about by the death of your brother?

Brian looks around helplessly. Hughie moves in, gets hold of his arm and pulls him to his feet.

SNOTTY REPORTER

You gonna answer the question?

THIRD REPORTER

You called a press conference.

A photographer steps in front of them. Hughie gives him a look that says 'back down or get a fat lip'.

HUGHIE

That'll do yer . . .

He steers him away.

SNOTTY REPORTER

You have a responsibility to answer these questions!

But they all troop out. Except for Luke, who turns on them.

LUKE

You people are really something, you know that? All you want is a few free drinks and a chance to tear people down. Those guys deserve a bit more respect! You bunch of wankers!

And he swaggers out.

INT. TRAILER. NIGHT

Guitars and cases all over the place. Tony, Ray and Luke are changing into their stage clothes. Karen enters.

KAREN

(*to Clare*)

See if you can find Beano, will you, love, I want everyone to hear this.

Clare hurries off. Les appears, cleaning his teeth.

LES

Hear what?

KAREN

Brian's not going on . . .

Silence.

Look, we knew it might happen. With or without him you're going to be OK. He just feels he could do without all that flak again, y'know?

The guys look thrown by this, especially Ray. There's an ominous rumble of thunder . . .

EXT. BACKSTAGE. NIGHT

Music pounds out from the band on-stage. Beano is still on the run, pushing oil drums between two rows of tents. He rounds a corner – and there she is, about twenty yards away.

WOMAN IN BLACK

Mr Baggot!

He stumbles backwards, falling to the ground. Behind him is the great hulking canvas canopy that encircles the rear of the stage.

The woman in black walks slowly towards him, picking her way carefully between cables and duckboards. Beano gets to his feet.

BEANO

Who are you?!

There's a curious, triumphant smile on her face as the chase comes to an end.

WOMAN

You were in the first band I ever saw. When I got home my father banned me from ever going to a rock concert again. He was a Methodist.

BEANO

So what d'you want from me?!

WOMAN

Quick, violent sex!

She flings aside her briefcase. Within seconds she's loosened his belt and unzipped his trousers, which fall around his ankles. Then she slides down out of sight.

Beano's face is a mixture of incredulity and relief.

BEANO

So you're not from the Inland Revenue, then?

EXT. AUDITORIUM. NIGHT

The audience is restless, whistling impatiently for the next act.

EXT. BACKSTAGE. NIGHT

Karen is in frantic conversation with Steve Greenblatt, surrounded by the Fruits.

KAREN

What can I tell you, Steve, I am minus a drummer!

STEVE

Look, don't pull this stroke on me, Karen, you're not going on after Quo! And if you don't go on now they're gonna get really ugly.

TONY

Listen to them! They're baying for our blood!

LES

Let's find another drummer. There's got to be a dozen in here –

He breaks off as Beano appears, sublimely unaware of any panic.

BEANO

Well, thank you very much for the loyalty, Les.

LES

Where have you been, you bollock?!

Karen is too relieved to be angry.

KAREN

It doesn't matter. Are you OK, Beano?

Beano has a shit-kicking grin on his face.

BEANO

I'm very OK, as a matter of fact . . . Well, shall we do this thing, then?

They start to file on-stage.

EXT. AUDITORIUM. NIGHT

The stage is in darkness and the crowd is slow-hand-clapping and chanting. Strange Fruit walk on-stage in darkness – Tony to the keyboards, Beano to the drums, Ray to the central mike. Les and Luke sling their guitars.

ANNOUNCER

OK, everyone. It's been far too long! So let me hear you give a great welcome to STRANGE FRUIT!!!

Tony signals Beano and the drums kick in. The crowd cheer as lights illuminate the band. Karen crosses her fingers.

This is the real deal at last. A vast stage with giant screens on either side, showing huge close-ups of the guys. Ray struts forward, with all the right moves, trying to will himself to believe it will be all right.

RAY

'Watch where you turn,
It might be today!
You lose your head
And just throw it away-hey-hey,
Oh yeah.
The wolf's at the . . .'

Suddenly Ray's throat closes and no words come out. He turns his back on the audience and walks away from the mike.

In the audience, Astrid reacts with alarm. The others watch anxiously. Tony and Les come in with the book.

TONY/LES

'Oh, you dangerous thing . . .'

In the wings Karen tries to will Ray to continue. But it's not going to happen. All his insecurities have peaked and he takes refuge at the rear of the stage. The band trail off raggedly.

The crowd react, more in embarrassment than hostility. No one seems to know what to do next.

It's Tony who saves the day. He starts to play the almost anthem-like opening chords of 'The Flame Still Burns'.

Ray looks at him – he didn't expect this. Nor did any of them. Tony eyes Les – OK? Les hesitates, then looks at Ray and nods – 'Go for it!'

Ray can't believe it. Les will let him sing that song? He moves to the mike.

RAY

'The Flame Still Burns'!

The audience applaud. Beano kicks in with the drums. And Ray returns Les's generosity, beckoning him forward to sing the opening lines alone.

LES

'I live a life that's surreal,
Where all that I feel I am learning . . .'

Luke has never played the song, doesn't know the key. Tony mouths 'E'! Ray joins Les and they sing together:

RAY/LES

'For life has been turned on the lathe,
Shaped with a flame that's still burning.'

Les's family hold their breath. So does Astrid.

EXT. BACKSTAGE AREA. NIGHT

Brian appears, as if drawn by the song. He's still wearing the old coat he used for gardening.

EXT. AUDITORIUM. NIGHT

The band are still singing.

RAY/LES

'And in time – it's all a sweet mystery,
When you shake the tree of temptation.'

EXT. BACKSTAGE AREA. NIGHT

Hughie sees Brian listening as the song continues. So does Karen. She watches as Hughie approaches Brian, holding his guitar out for him to slip his arms through the strap. He shakes his head, no, but Hughie persists.

RAY/LES
(*off-screen*)

'And I . . . I know the fear and the cost
Of a paradise lost in frustration . . .'

Karen approaches Brian now, offering him the sixpence she still wears round her wrist.

'And the flame still burns!
It's there in my soul,
For that unfinished goal . . .'

Brian takes the sixpence, maybe remembering the moment when he gave it to her all those years ago. Their eyes lock.

'And the flame still burns!
From a glimmer and then
It lights up again in my life.'

Les nudges Ray, who turns, following his look towards the wings.

Right on cue, Brian makes his entrance. He kicks off the instrumental break with a beautiful guitar lick, using the sixpence for a pick.

The crowd sees him and a response ripples round the stadium like electricity. Ray goes down on his knees in tribute. Finally, the band is complete! Brian's chords fill the night air, echoing over the vast sea of faces.

Close on Karen in the wings. She makes eye contact with Tony and wipes a tear from her eye. This is why she did it. This is rock 'n' roll and nothing else comes close. She gives Clare an ecstatic hug.

'But my life has no language of love,
No word from above is appearing.
Oh, but time – and time is a fire
That's stoked with reason,
And hope and believing.'

Ray and Les beckon Brian forward and the three of them sing together:

RAY/LES/BRIAN

'And the flame still burns – yeah!
Yes, it's there in my soul,
For that unfinished goal,
And the flame still burns!
From a glimmer and then
It lights up again in my life,
Keep it rolling,
Keep that flame still burning.'

There's an ominous rumble of thunder and, for a moment, the sky is lit by lightning. Karen looks skyward.

KAREN

Don't you dare!!

RAY/LES/BRIAN

'Keep a-rolling around,
The world keeps turning – yeah!'

Hughie's voice completes the story:

HUGHIE

(*voice-over*)

I was wrong about God. Turns out He likes that 1970s stuff after all. So it didn't piss down and they played four encores. And with the Almighty in their corner, who knows what might happen?

The band plays on and the fans cheer.

And how will the Fruits conspire to bollix things up this time around? We wait with baited breath!

The camera pulls back, further and further, and music continues through the end titles.

Then – when the final title rolls and there are only cleaners left in the cinema, and people looking for their glasses under the seat, we hear:

RAY

(*voice-over*)

Oh, I've got one. Uh, Tom Petty and the Heartbreakers.

BEANO

(*voice-over*)

Oh, yeah, I had one with 'heart'. Gerry and the Pacemakers!

Fade out.

Credits

CAST

TONY COSTELLO	Stephen Rea
HUGHIE, THE ROADIE	Billy Connolly
LES WICKES	Jimmy Nail
BEANO BAGGOT	Timothy Spall
RAY SIMMS	Bill Nighy
KAREN KNOWLES	Juliet Aubrey
ASTRID SIMMS	Helena Bergström
BRIAN LOVELL	Bruce Robinson
LUKE SHAND	Hans Matheson
CLARE KNOWLES	Rachel Stirling
NEIL GAYDON	Phil Daniels
LIMO DRIVER	Phil Davis
LADY IN BLACK	Frances Barber
ANNABEL	Zoë Ball
GARY	Andy Nichol
HOCKNEY	Frances Magee
NOT MORRISSEY	Justin Gratton
JASON	Delroy Atkinson
STEVE GREENBLATT	Julian Simms
WAITRESS 1	Margaret Blackmore
APPRENTICE	Chris Wild
PIZZA BOY	Dean Lennox Kelly
DUTCH KID	Mackenzie Crook
DUTCH HITCHHIKER	Donna Air
YOUNG KAREN	Virginia Clay
YOUNG HUGHIE	Luke Garrett
YOUNG BEANO	Sean Mackenzie
YOUNG RAY	Rupert Penry-Jones
YOUNG LES	Alex Palmer
YOUNG BRIAN	Matthew Finney

YOUNG KEITH	Lee Williams
CLUB OWNER	Ralph Vandijk
DUTCH RECEPTIONIST	Sabina Michael
PROMOTER	Kerry Shale
DUTCH LOCAL	Steve Ubels
CLIVE	Danny Webb
TAX WOMAN	Anita Carey
FEMALE REPORTER	Daisy Donovan

THE FILM-MAKERS

Director	Brian Gibson
Writers	Dick Clement
	Ian La Frenais
Producer	Amanda Marmot
Executive Producers	Dick Clement
	Ian La Frenais
Line Producer	Steve Clark-Hall
Music Producers	Clive Langer and
	Alan Winstanley
Music Supervisors	Steve Dagger
	Tarquin Gotch
Music Director	Gary Kemp
Director of Photography	Ashley Rowe
Editor	Peter Boyle
Production Designer	Max Gottlieb
Sound Recordist	Colin Nicolson
Costume Designer	Caroline Harris
Casting Director	Gail Stevens
Composer	Clive Langer
Hair Designer	Jan Archibald
Make-up Designer	Morag Ross
Production Supervisor	Waldo Roeg
Post Production Supervisor	Stephen Law
Script Supervisor	Liz West
Production Accountant	Richard Hyland
Location Manager	Sam Breckman
1st Assistant Director	Simon Moseley
2nd Assistant	Sallie Hard

3rd Assistant	Ben Burt
Art Director	Sarah Jane Cornish
Set Decorator	Rebecca Alleway
Production Buyer	Anna Lynch-Robinson
Assistant Art Director	Grant Armstrong
Art Department Assistant	Taylor Huggins
Art Department Assistant	Liliana Cifonelli
Property Master	John Mills
Dressing Props	Michael Mills
Props Dresser	Terry Wood
Standby Props	Gus Lipton
2nd Standby Prop	Paul Cheesman
Storekeeper	Stan Cook
Costume Supervisor	Dee Walsh
Wardrobe Master	Julian Day
Assistant Costume	Emily Bradbury
Costume Assistant	Catherine Birchall
Make-up Artist	Sally Jaye
Make-up Assistant	Pauline Fahily
Hair Artist	Astrid Schikorra
Hair Assistant	Tapio Salmi
2nd Unit Director	Adrian Sibley
2nd Unit Camera	Matt Gray
Focus Puller	Ian Clark
2nd Focus Puller	Julian Bucknall
Clapper Loader	Steve Laws
2nd Clapper Loader	Matthew Woolf
Camera Trainee	Ed Wright
Video Assist Trainee	Colleen Webley
Boom Operator	Tony Cook
3rd Sound Man	Noel Thompson
Key Grip	Kevin David Higgins
2nd Grip	Bob Langridge
Gaffer	John Donaghue
Best Boy	William Tracey
Genny Driver	Gary Donoghue
Truck Driver	David Wall
Electrician	Darren Harvey
Construction Manager	Mike Houseman

Charge Hand	Paul Fogarty
Stagehand	Seter Agbaba
Painter	Mark Adams
Painter	Guy Rutter
Carpenter	Ian Bee
Carpenter	John Drury
Apprentice Carpenter	John Walpole
Standby Carpenter	Leon McCarthy
Standby Stagehand	Gary Davis
Standby Rigger	Andy Ormisher
Stills Photographer	Alex Bailey
Assistant Editor	Liz Roe
Unit Driver	Harry E. Smith
Unit Driver	Tony Jayes
Unit Driver	Nigel Birtchnell
Unit Driver	Terry Reece
Unit Driver	Steve Clark
Facility Captain	Mac Maclean
Make-up Driver	John Morris
Construction Standby Driver	Kim Worley
Camera Truck	Townley Knott
Wardrobe Driver	Michael Fitchdining
Bus Driver	Tiny Topping
Honey Wagon	Dean Taylor
Minibus Driver	Simon Randall
Publicity	Corbett & Keene
Unit Publicist	Linda Gamble
Stunt Coordinator	Nicholas Powell
Stand In	James Linton
Stand In	Clare Chrysler
Stand In	Joe Lacey
Unit Nurse	Nicky Jarvis
Special Effects Supervisor	Stuart Brisdon
Production Company Holland	The Filmstones BV
Caterers	Woodhall Catering